**W9-BWD-418**

The
Baker Creek
Vegan
Cookbook

ALSO BY JERE & EMILEE GETTLE

The Heirloom Life Gardener

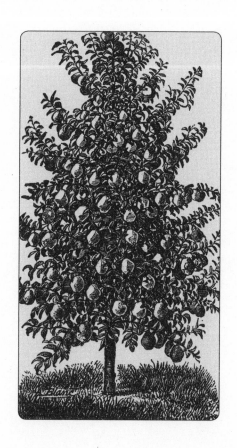

Jere & Emilee Gettle

with

Adeena Sussman

The
Baker Creek

Vegan Cookbook

Traditional Ways to Cook,
Preserve, and Eat the Harvest

hachette
BOOKS

NEW YORK   BOSTON

Copyright © 2012 Jeremiath C. Gettle and Emilee Freie Gettle

Hachette Book Group supports the right to free expression and the value of copyright. The purpose of copyright is to encourage writers and artists to produce the creative works that enrich our culture.

The scanning, uploading, and distribution of this book without permission is a theft of the author's intellectual property. If you would like permission to use material from the book (other than for review purposes), please contact permissions@hbgusa.com. Thank you for your support of the author's rights.

Hachette Books
Hachette Book Group
1290 Avenue of the Americas, New York, NY 10104
hachettebooks.com
twitter.com/hachettebooks

Originally published by Hyperion.
First Hachette Books edition: January 2017

Hachette Books is a division of Hachette Book Group, Inc.
The Hachette Books name and logo are trademarks of Hachette Book Group, Inc.

The publisher is not responsible for websites (or their content) that are not owned by the publisher.

Library of Congress Cataloging-in-Publication Data

Gettle, Jere.
  The Baker Creek vegan cookbook: traditional ways to cook, preserve, and eat the harvest/Jere and Emilee Gettle, with Adeena Sussman.—1st ed.
      p. cm.
  ISBN 978-1-4013-1061-5
  1. Vegan cooking. 2. Canning and preserving. 3. Cooking (Vegetables) 4. Cooking (Fruit) 5. Cookbooks. I. Gettle, Emilee. II. Sussman, Adeena. III. Title.
  TX837.G397 2012
  641.5'636—dc23

                                                        2012007757

BOOK DESIGN BY SHUBHANI SARKAR

ISBNs: 978-1-4013-1061-5 (trade paperback), 978-1-4013-0475-1 (ebook)

Printed in the United States of America

LSC-C

10 9 8 7 6 5 4 3

TO OUR DAUGHTER

Sasha

who finds joy in the garden
and in the kitchen

Contents

The
Baker Creek
Vegan
Cookbook

Introduction

I live with my wife, Emilee, and our young daughter, Sasha, on a 176-acre parcel of property in Mansfield, Missouri, we call Baker Creek. All around us, on land that was passed down to us from my parents, we grow organic, heirloom produce on a patchwork of fields. Rarely a day goes by when I don't find myself in the field marveling at a new shape, color, or texture I've never encountered before. I don't think it would be an overstatement to say that vegetables are my life . . . and during harvest season, Emilee would certainly agree!

Through our company, the Baker Creek Heirloom Seed Company, we have an ongoing relationship with hundreds of thousands of gardeners and farmers who are passionate about growing and eating things that they can feel good about. It's hard, exciting work, and we love it.

As far as I'm concerned, the kitchen is a natural extension of the field. My love of good food dates back nearly as far as my knowledge of farming and gardening. Being from a family of homesteaders based around the Idaho-Oregon border, I have memories of everyone taking an active role in raising produce, either as a hobby or as a career. We all had mud on our shoes, dirt under our nails, and freckles on our noses—and it suited us just fine.

We moved around a few times when I was young, but farming and gardening were our constants, with the roots we planted in the ground providing the roots we needed to settle down and get comfortable. It just wasn't home unless things were sprouting in the garden and in our fields, and until we were turning the fruits of our labor into soul-satisfying meals.

Naturally, all of this planting and growing meant a lot of good eating. My mom, Debbie, was—and is—a great cook, who always kept things simple and delicious. My parents almost never went out to eat, because it was expensive, but also because it didn't fit our chosen, stick-to-the-farm lifestyle.

That meant homemade biscuits for breakfast, with jam in any number of flavors; casseroles made with different kinds of beans, potatoes, and tomatoes; burgers ground from meat that my dad hunted, topped with sauerkraut pickled from our very own cabbages; and double-crusted apple pies dusted with sanding sugar. Add to the equation two grandmothers—Opal and Bertha—and a slew of other kitchen-comfortable relatives, and the result was one well-fed little boy.

From an early age I took for granted something that, until recently, was becoming forgotten to many Americans: that the connection between the land under our feet and the food on our table is one of the greatest stories of American history.

My childhood was marked by long, sunny afternoons foraging wild asparagus along the creek banks near our homestead, the green pointy tips pushing up through the dirt. Mom steamed them before we ate them hot from the pot with our fingers, trying not to burn our hands or our tongues. We also spent hours plucking huckleberries in the hills, then would gorge ourselves before surrendering some of the inky berries for pancakes that we'd make either on an open fire while camping or in our farm kitchen.

I also really enjoyed foraging in the wild for food. We'd often find meadow mushrooms in the fields, which my mom would sauté for dinner. In the Ozarks, I searched the leaf-covered grounds in the woods near our home for treasured morels.

The end of the summer also brought epic sessions of preserving and "putting up," an all-hands-on-deck affair that would result in hundreds of cans, jars, and frozen ziplock bags of garden-raised produce that we then feasted on all winter long. And come colder weather, our root cellar, where we kept yams, potatoes of all kinds, apples, rutabagas, turnips, and parsnips, became our go-to larder for delicious staples.

I can still feel the sun on my neck as I went out into the summer garden with my dad to find more watermelons than any one family could ever eat. Sunshine-hued Orangelos, red-fleshed Crimson Sweets, and yellow-centered Tender Sweets—we would crack them open right there in the field and eat the sweet hearts straight out of their green rinds, sugary juice running down our faces and making our hands sticky.

At that point, people—myself included—really weren't aware of the potential of heirloom produce. The significance of historic varieties was something we either took for granted or just let slip by. Some of our seeds came from grandparents or neighbors, which we would in turn save and pass along to our friends. Through the passage of years, I started to notice my favorite varieties disappearing from seed catalogs, and it was at that point I grasped the importance of preserving our agricultural heritage by saving and passing on heirloom seed varieties to keep them from becoming extinct.

I was three years old when I planted my first heirloom seeds—they were scallop squash selected by my dad. He helped me put them in the ground, and I eagerly awaited the day when the tiny green squash plants pushed through our rich soil.

A few months later, when I found a bumpy, wavy-edged vegetable lying under the shade of the giant squash vine, I was hooked. Every year my dad would take me into the field to help plant and harvest our crops—and to get my own seed selections into the soil.

When I first picked up a knife and started cooking for myself, at the age of twelve, things just came naturally. I guess I had a head start, since practically every meal I'd eaten up to that point was eaten at home, or at least had been made by someone I knew. I enjoyed coming up with new recipes—or adjusting old family favorites to my personal taste—all the while experimenting with techniques I'd read about in my favorite cooking magazines.

Ever since I can remember, I've been fascinated by how people live—and what they eat—in different parts of the world. I pored over the pages of *National Geographic* and other travel magazines to learn about far-flung places, dreaming of traveling overseas and tasting the local specialties. Whenever we were at a new or larger supermarket, I'd lose track of time studying the kumquats, star fruits, and other things I'd never seen before, then I'd go home and read anything I could get my hands on that would explain what I had been feasting my eyes on.

It was around this time that I also started collecting heirloom seeds as a hobby, and joined the Seed Savers Exchange, where I learned about the threat to our seeds from multinational corporations using biotechnology to manipulate crops, plants, and seeds. I printed my first heirloom seed catalog in 1998 as a teenager's hobby, and pretty soon business was booming. I suppose it was partly timing, but I just followed my passion for the seeds I loved and the rest unfolded, as they say, organically.

Today, our Baker Creek Heirloom Seed catalog has a circulation of 300,000 households, people who look to us to learn about recently reintroduced heirloom varieties and the ways that maintaining diversity through farming and gardening is a win-win proposition in terms of nutrition, taste, and social responsibility. (You can learn more about heirloom gardening and our company in our first book, *The Heirloom Life Gardener*.)

We sell upward of 2 million seed packets a year, and I know from our very active Web followers that people are using what they grow in the kitchen. Things simply taste better when they come from your own garden, and that's also the only way you can guarantee that your produce is being grown to your moral, ethical, and culinary standards.

Until recently, it seemed that Americans were suffering from the Incredible Shrinking Garden. Standard supermarkets offered the same rotation of lifeless, colorless vegetables year-round, and people had lost touch with what is exciting about growing and gardening: its endless variety. Thankfully, many changes are afoot. Farmers' markets, farm-to-table restaurants, community-supported agriculture (CSAs), and just a return to a more vegetable-based diet make us feel like we're doing something right. I think that's the real reason what we're doing at Baker Creek is taking off—it's simply the right thing to do. And sometimes, it really is true that the best food in the world can be as straightforward as a tomato slice on a thick slab of home-baked bread, the whole juicy lot sprinkled with salt.

Although I love an unadorned crispy apple or crunchy carrot as much as the next person, this book is about how to take that bounty and transform it into delicious meals. We'd like to get people to start forming lasting connections between heirloom produce and heirloom recipes—making both into treasured family property that gets passed down from generation to generation.

Here in Missouri, we always plant more than we can use. This year, for instance, I've got nearly seventy varieties of eggplant growing, from sweet Malaysian Dark Reds to globe-like Italians.

Growing more than we needed led us to open a pay-as-you-can restaurant at Baker Creek in 2009 that is rapidly becoming a gathering place for like-minded people from the neighborhood and beyond, as well as a place to feed the expanding Baker Creek staff.

It's ironic, but the area around our farm is dotted with fast-food restaurants and strip malls. If it doesn't involve a deep-fryer, it can be hard to find. Since there aren't a lot of healthy food options, we decided to take matters into our own hands and use the restaurant as a way to share our passion for heirlooms.

As more and more people visit our village (in addition to our seed store, we've got a blacksmith shop, a seed museum, and a bakery), they want to taste the fruits of our labor. We prepare one or two main dishes a day, often inspired by our love of Asian food and the way certain cultures make healthy, seasonal eating so simple and seductive. I've had the privilege of traveling in Cambodia,

Thailand, and Burma, and there the vegetables aren't the supporting players—they're usually the stars.

On one of my first dates with Emilee we ate pad thai, and we have a tasty version that we serve at the restaurant. But our recipes aren't limited to Southeast Asian cuisine. We'll serve Emilee's sweet potato casserole or surprisingly moist eggplant cake, my mom's sundried tomato bread—it really depends on our whim, what's in the garden, and what we think would taste best, based on availability and our cravings. We're still working out the kinks, but we're proud of the work we're doing at the restaurant.

The recipes in this book have been adapted and developed from a variety of sources, but with one common purpose: to share with people just how diverse heirloom produce can be.

My family has a long history of vegetarianism, and since my early teens, I have been vegan. So throughout the book, you will learn about the clever substitutes we keep in our pantry to ensure that our food not only tastes great, but also aspires to a healthy lifestyle. I have included recipes that have been passed down through generations of vegetarians, with each new generation perfecting the recipes and making them their own. By making vegetarian meals starring heirloom produce, you'll be eating whole foods, all the while introducing healthy new ingredients into your diet. You'll also be writing your own personal page in American food history; here's hoping it's a tasty journey.

Canning and Preserving

At all three of our stores—in Missouri, California, and Connecticut—we've been getting more and more requests for information and advice about canning and preserving, and we can't say we're surprised. As gardeners learn to love their many varieties of homegrown heirlooms, it only makes sense to find ways to make them last year-round. I come from a family of canners, as well, but for more detailed information and instructions, I'm handing over the reins to my wife, Emilee, whose family has been canning for generations, and who herself has a passion for "putting up" fruits and vegetables.

One of the things I look forward to most come winter is reaching into my pantry to find row upon row of gleaming jars filled with juicy, peak-ripe tomatoes, crisp beans, garlicky pickles, and other examples of summer's bounty, captured behind glass and waiting to be enjoyed by family and friends.

There's something great about how this process completes the early gardening cycle—and keeps the promise of summer alive as the wind whispers through the walls of our old farmhouse and the snow gently falls outside.

After all the work is done, and everything is sealed and labeled for the winter, I sit back, breathe a sweet sigh of accomplishment, and reflect on all that we gained in a season.

During canning season at my house, the kitchen is filled with bubbling pots and the sound of clinking and clanking glass jars, all waiting to be filled with our homegrown treasures: the veggies plucked from our own gardens. The yearly ritual of preserving the garden's abundance brings back warm memories for me. I'll never forget learning this timeless kitchen skill from my grandmother, Nellie, and my mother, Lyn, who began teaching me how to can and preserve when I was quite young. Our laughter during preserving days echoed from row to row in the field and joyously kept time with the click-clack of the pressure canner.

This chapter will cover the basics of canning, freezing, and drying, the way that I do it in my home. There is much to learn about preserving, and this chapter is just a primer—a springboard to get you excited as you embark on this wonderful pastime.

When I was a teenager in northern Missouri, I spent the early summer mornings in the gardens with my mother, picking tomatoes, green beans, and okra, while our lazy cat, Sassy, supervised the proceedings. Once we had a few bushel baskets or wheelbarrows filled, we'd wheel them back up to the house, park the bounty outside the back door to the kitchen, and the assembly line would begin. Being in a 4-H club, I entered my own canned concoctions in the county fair—and was always surprised and thrilled when they were occasionally decorated with a blue ribbon.

The History of Canning

Ever since Napoleon struggled to feed his hungry army, there's been a record of people canning to preserve their food. "An army marches on its stomach," said Napoleon, whose creative solution to a dire food shortage was to offer a reward of 12,000 francs to the first clever individual to devise an inexpensive way to preserve food. A brewer and confectioner named Nicolas Appert came up with the answer. He'd discovered that food didn't spoil when tightly sealed in jars. He didn't know why, exactly—it took Louis Pasteur to solve the mystery some fifty years later—but this was one of the most significant developments in food history before the advent of refrigeration. *Merci,* Napoleon!

Canning

Canning destroys microorganisms that cause food spoilage by heating sterilized jars and creating a vacuum seal. There are two main types of canning: Water-bath and pressure. **Water-bath canning** is ideal for foods with a high level of acidity (specifically, a pH of 4.6 or less), such as berries, peaches, and nectarines. **Pressure canning**, which we don't use for this book, is typically for starchy foods with a low acid content (pH of 4.7 or higher).

If processed correctly, home-canned foods can maintain the same level of food safety as commercially manufactured products. When you're just getting started canning and preserving, it's important not to stray too far from a time-tested recipe, so you can maintain an environment that prevents bacterial growth and reduces changes in appearance such as discoloration and texture. Don't take shortcuts: Follow each step in the canning process from start to finish, cutting no corners, so you end up with food products you can be proud of.

The main point I want to convey is that canning is something everyone can enjoy. Whether you live in the city or the country, whether you have access to a grocery store, an expanse of crop fields, or a farmers' market—it doesn't matter. Canning empowers us to preserve food at its peak for use at a later time. It connects us with a time-honored ritual and allows us to carry on this tradition with our own loved ones.

At first glance, the process might seem complicated, but don't be intimidated. Over time, the process becomes familiar, kind of like making your favorite recipe for dinner.

Equipment

The most important step when canning is organization. Have all your equipment ready before you begin the process and things will go much more smoothly.

Here's what you'll need:

WATER-BATH CANNER

Many companies sell pots that are specifically labeled as "water-bath canners," but any large pot with a tight-fitting lid will do the trick. I prefer to work with a 21-quart pot, which has a dual purpose: to both sterilize your jars and create a water-bath environment. You can buy the canner new, but oftentimes they are available at secondhand stores. Just make sure the one you buy has a tight-fitting lid.

JARS AND LIDS

Only use jars designed specifically for home canning. New jars come with lids and bands; the jars and bands are reusable, but the lids aren't; lids help create the airtight seal essential to well-preserved fruits and vegetables, and they can be used only once.

Before using, carefully inspect the lid and lip of each jar for dents, nicks or chips (or, in older jars, bubbles). Discard any damaged lids, as even a small imperfection could prevent your jar from sealing properly, which can make food dangerous. The metal can become damaged, rusty, or sharp, so watch carefully for that as well.

CANNING RACK

I've burned my hands one too many times by not using one of these handy racks, which can be inserted into your canner or pot. If you buy a new canner, definitely buy one with a rack. In a pinch, my grandmother Nellie taught me to put a dish towel on the bottom of the canner, which is a great buffer for glass jars and minimizes the clanking during the boiling phase.

FUNNEL, TONGS, AND MAGNETIC LID LIFTER

I call these the "three musketeers" of canning. A wide-mouthed funnel prevents splatters and splashing while you fill your jars with produce and brine. Special tongs designed to grip jars by their necks save your hands from burns while allowing you to handle the piping-hot jars after they've been boiling. A magnetic lid lifter, essentially a stick with a magnet affixed to the end, is a cool invention; I had one and always used it growing up. You'll use it to remove lids from hot water after you sterilize them.

DISH TOWELS

Dish towels are the workhorses of the canning kitchen. If food residue is on the rim when you put the lid on, your jar will not seal properly. Use a clean, damp dish towel to wipe off the rim of the jar after you fill it up. When you take your jars out of the canner, use towels to alleviate the dramatic change in temperature while they rest. You'll need a few: Place the jars on top of a towel when you remove them, and cover them with another towel to release heat gradually and provide for an optimal seal.

TIMER

Lots can happen when you're canning—who knows? You might even be preserving multiple items at once. Put a timer to good use, as a friendly reminder to achieve the proper processing time.

Water-Bath Canning

STEP 1: PREP

Cleanliness, organization, and careful preparation are key here. Your workspace, hands, and anything that is near the food you're working with must be very clean. Wash hands thoroughly. Sanitize all countertops. Gather all equipment and organize. Make sure you have all ingredients needed before you get started, and take into account that canning and preserving require multiple steps, such as blanching or peeling tomatoes and stone fruits, or salting vegetables such as cabbage for preservation.

STEP 2: STERILIZE JARS

To sterilize your jars, place a canning rack into the water-bath canner, fill halfway with water and bring to a low boil. Insert jars, one by one, into the water-filled canner. Cover and return to a low boil, making sure jars are filled with water. The jars must boil for at least ten minutes to be sterilized. Keep jars in water until you are ready to use them to maintain sterilization.

STEP 3: STERILIZE LIDS

While your jars are simmering, fill a skillet halfway with boiling water. Add lids and let simmer over medium heat at least ten minutes. Do not allow the water for the lids to boil too vigorously; this could harm the gasket and jeopardize the seal of your jar.

STEP 4: PREP RECIPE

Mix whatever ingredients you're using as directed by the recipe.

STEP 5: FILL JARS

Finally—the fun part! To fill the jars, remove one at a time from the canner with tongs, pour any water out of each jar, and place on individual saucers covered with a clean, dry washcloth (this prevents temperature shock as the hot jar is transferred to a surface in preparation for filling). Place your wide-mouthed funnel in the sterilized jar and fill it up by the spoonful or just pour it in there, depending on the contents.

If you do a lot of canning, you'll eventually find out that jars drop, slip, and break. They even explode in some circumstances. A cold enamel table, for example, is not a good place to put a piping hot glass jar. Pop! Glass and food goes everywhere. Use a dry cloth-lined saucer to help jars acclimate after they are lifted from the boiling water.

STEP 6: LEAVE THE PROPER AMOUNT OF HEADSPACE

The contents of the jar will expand during the canning process, so leave some headspace between the lid and the food that is being prepared. The rule is a half inch of headspace for whole vegetables and sauces, and a quarter inch of headspace for spreads and juices. This step is very important, because if too little headspace is left, food will seep through the lid and destroy the seal. Likewise, if there's too much headspace, too much oxygen will be left in the jar, which might lead to discoloration, bacterial growth, or an insufficient vacuum.

High-Altitude Canning

If you are canning at a high altitude, your processing times need to be adjusted. For water baths, give it one extra minute per thousand feet for recipes with processing times less than twenty minutes and provide two extra minutes per thousand feet for processing times exceeding twenty minutes.

STEP 7: ELIMINATE AIR BUBBLES

When working with pickles or whole vegetables, you often will get air bubbles after you pour the hot brine into the jar. To remove them, poke a dull dinner knife, small offset spatula, or the handle of a wooden spoon all the way to the base of the jar several times. This may cause the liquid level to go down as air bubbles are popped, and you may need to add more liquid to maintain adequate headspace.

STEP 8: PUT A LID ON IT

Using a clean, damp cloth, wipe any food residue from the rim of the jar. Remove lids from simmering water. Place a lid on each jar, then seal with a band. Make sure the band is sealed securely but not too securely; there needs to be some slack to allow jars to process properly.

STEP 9: BOIL

Remove, fill, and place jars back into the hot water canner, repeating the process one at a time until the canner is filled with jars, still allowing for two inches of water to cover the jars.

Add water to the canner as needed to cover jars, then bring to a boil and cover pot. You will need to maintain a rolling boil for your recipe's specified time to ensure a proper seal. Start the timer as soon as you have reached a rolling boil. You might need to add more hot water during the process, so keep an eye on the pot as the water evaporates.

STEP 10: SEAL IT

Once the timer goes off, turn off the burner and let your pot rest, uncovered, for about five minutes. Using jar-lifting tongs, remove each jar and transport it to the towel-covered table or countertop using a washcloth-covered saucer. Allow a little space between jars for airflow and cover with another clean towel. Don't be tempted to fiddle with the bands, as this can disturb the seal. As tempting as it is to touch them, let the jars rest for about twelve hours. It's music to my ears to hear each lid give that distinctive *ping!* sound as I clean up the kitchen.

STEP 11: WATCH THE LID

Once you've canned and cooled your jars, check seals after twenty-four hours to make sure the lids have inverted and developed suction. If your jarred items are meant to sit for a week or two to pickle or develop flavor,

check the seals again before opening to make sure they're still inverted.

STEP 12: LISTEN FOR THE POP

Once you unscrew the seal and open the lid, listen for the distinctive *pop!* sound, which ensures freshness and that preserving has been a success. If you don't hear it, sadly, I'd recommend not using the food you've preserved. After you've initially opened a jar, refrigerate and use within a few days.

Freezing

With our busy lifestyle, freezing is a quick and easy way to preserve summer's bounty. My freezers are stocked year-round with frozen peppers, green beans, blueberries, peaches, zucchini, freezer pickles, tomatoes, and other goodies. It takes some time to put it all together, but what a blessing it is to find neatly labeled bags in our freezers waiting to be prepared into our favorite dish at the restaurant or in our own kitchen in the dead of winter! There are some drawbacks to freezing versus canning—such as power outages. However, freezing does seem to maintain the crispness and texture that canning at times may not.

You can freeze produce in plastic freezer bags, reusable plastic freezer boxes, or specially made freezer jars (the latter are available in most stores with a canning section, or at hardware stores).

Vegetables require blanching: Wash vegetables and plunge into boiling water, or

---

Canning Basics: Jars

I love using distinctive, antique blue Mason jars, which make gifts of preserved produce look extra special. I buy them at estate sales in the country, where they're often available by the box for just a few dollars—or on eBay, where they show up with regularity. Always purchase new lids for antique jars each time you use them for canning. Before you can with them, slide your finger across the rim of each jar to check for nicks, bubbles in the glass, or cracks. If you come across any imperfections, do not use for canning, as the seal may be faulty and could affect the safety of the finished product. But even if you can't use them for canning, they're great for storing herbs, teas, or grains.

steam for a few minutes before transferring to an ice water bath to stop the cooking process. This technique enhances color—especially in green vegetables—and ensures a great tasting and attractive finished product. Blanching times vary, depending on the vegetable to be frozen.

Bag or box your blanched vegetables, then label by contents and date of packaging. To ensure that your vegetables don't clump together in the freezer, bag them in plastic freezer bags and lay flat on cookie sheets.

To freeze herbs such as basil, rosemary, thyme, and oregano, wash them. Then mince them up and fill the compartments of an ice cube tray halfway with the herbs. Fill the tray with water and freeze. Once frozen, pop the cubes into a plastic freezer bag so you can use them in winter recipes such as homemade Italian dishes.

GREEN BEANS

Step 1: Wash beans thoroughly and snap off the stem end of the bean. Using a paring knife, trim any blemishes.

Step 2: Fill a large stockpot with water. Set pot on stove and bring water to a boil. Do not add salt, as this will diminish the quality of the frozen beans.

Step 3: Once the water comes to a rolling boil, drop beans in and allow to blanch for three minutes.

Step 4: Remove from hot water and shock in an ice water bath.

Step 5: Once cool, drain, dry, and pack into freezer bags or boxes; label accordingly.

ZUCCHINI

We always have an abundance of zucchini, so I like to grind up my extra bounty in the food processor and freeze it for later use in zucchini breads, which make for wonderful holiday gifts.

Step 1: Wash zucchini. Trim stems and blossom, then cut into two-inch pieces.

Step 2: Process zucchini in small batches in a food processor until smooth.

Step 3: Spoon into freezer bags and label.

Drying

Growing up, I loved using our dehydrator with my mother. It was so much fun and made the house smell great. One year, my parents and I cultivated such a huge okra patch that after exhausting every recipe for cooking, canning, and freezing, we still had a basketful left. My creative mother decided to slice and dehydrate it. We began adding the dried okra to soups and as a crunchy topping for Caesar salads. We used it in lieu of bacon bits. My mother loves it crumbled into tomato soup—something I ate at lunchtime many afternoons growing up.

The process of dehydrating food has existed for thousands of years. Before the invention of refrigeration, people salted meats and vegetables to extract moisture from food that would cause it to decompose; food was also dried in the sun.

Early American homesteaders strung bean pods to hang them from the rafters and bundled garlands of peppers and herbs as reminders of the harvest and a blessed reassurance that there was always one more meal available to serve. The way we eat and access our food supply may have changed radically, but that doesn't mean you can't preserve your produce as they did years ago.

For a more modern alternative, you can make your own dehydrator, like Jere's parents did in Oregon, or you can purchase a new one. Either way, dehydrating is a simple process that yields amazing results.

You can dehydrate vegetables grown in your garden such as peppers, tomatoes (I love whole cherry-type tomatoes), beans, pumpkin, okra, beets, carrots, broccoli, cauliflower, peas, corn, and others. Be sure to choose blemish-free produce for optimal results. The key to properly drying food is to reduce the moisture content to a point where the produce will not mold or become an inviting abode for bacteria; properly dried vegetables are actually quite brittle.

Blanching some vegetables prior to dehydrating is recommended since it inhibits enzyme growth, which could cause spoilage.

Always slice the vegetables uniformly and place on dehydrator trays in a single layer, being careful to leave room between vegetables.

These days you can buy a thermostatically controlled dehydrator, which eliminates drying-time guesswork. Simply dehydrate your vegetables at the temperature and time recommended in the manual and you're good to go. To be on the safe side, I like to do my own quality control by removing a few dehydrated vegetables from the tray and allowing them to cool completely. If they are brittle and no beads of moisture escape when you snap them, they're ready.

You can store dried vegetables for up to a year by using this method. More likely, you'll have empty jars before the year is up. They're simply so good, and if you have kids in the house, not only will they love watching the dehydrating process, but they will devour the finished product. And don't forget that you can also dry your favorite herbs for the winter.

Here are a few of my favorites:

GREEN BEANS
Trim ends and cut into one-inch pieces. Steam or blanch in boiling water for four minutes, drain, and dry according to your own dehydrator's manual or until brittle.

BEETS
Wash beets and place in a large saucepan, then cook in boiling water until tender. Slip skin off with a paring knife. Cut into quarter-inch rounds and dry for ten to twelve hours, until brittle.

CARROTS
Wash and peel, then cut into thin slices. Dehydrate for six to twelve hours, until brittle.

SWEET PEPPERS

Wash, seed, and slice peppers into quarter-inch strips. Dehydrate twelve to eighteen hours, or until brittle. Once they are dry, add as a crunchy addition to salads or throw into soups.

POTATOES

Wash, then thinly slice. Dehydrate for six to twelve hours, or until brittle.

TOMATOES

Wash tomatoes. Blanch in boiling water for four minutes. Use a paring knife to remove skin, stem, and core. If using small tomatoes, leave whole and skip blanching. If using larger varieties, cut into quarter-inch slices. Dried tomatoes are a zesty addition to salads, sandwiches, sauces, and marinades.

HERBS

Gather herbs into a bundle, tie with a pretty ribbon, and hang to dry for later use.

Dehydrating Tips

* Always choose vegetables that are at the peak of freshness and free from blemishes or bruises.
* Chop pieces into a uniform size and arrange in a single layer. Be careful that veggies don't touch each other while drying.
* Store dehydrated vegetables in an air-tight glass jar or container to keep moisture out.
* Eat rehydrated veggies right away or they will spoil.
* Spray your dehydrator trays with a thin coating of cooking spray or rub them down with a little olive oil. This will prevent the dried produce from sticking to your trays and avoid lengthy cleanup.
* If you live in a humid climate, that will affect drying time. Refer to your dehydrator manual for details about adusting times for each vegetable.

Kitchen Staples

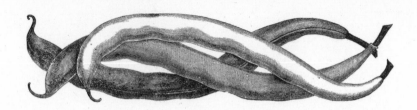

Cooking 100-percent naturally and without animal products means using some special ingredients to replace non-vegan items. These are some of the things we always keep on hand for baking and cooking. Most are available at health food stores and specialty grocers, through food cooperatives, or online. Increasingly, you can even find some of them at regular stores.

BUYING ORGANIC AND NON-GMO

We feel that it is imperative to know what is in the food we are eating, so for any food product that we don't grow or produce on our own land, we buy non-GMO and organic. If you're unsure of what food products and brands contain GMOs (genetically modified organisms), visit *www.responsibletechnology.org/buy-non-gmo* and download their non-GMO shopping list.

COCONUT MILK

A can of full-fat coconut milk opens up a world of possibilities for non-dairy cooks and bakers. Use it to thicken sauces, enrich curries, enhance baked goods, or make great beverages. Chill it for a few hours, then use the solidified coconut cream as the base for a rich whipped topping.

COCONUT OIL

In the debate over healthy oils, coconut oil comes out a winner. It does have saturated fat, but it's an all-natural oil that, in its natural, harder, room-temperature form, can stand in for butter or shortening in pastry recipes, with super-flaky results. It can also withstand moderate to high heat for sautéing and stir-frying, and it's got a surprisingly mild flavor. Look for the least refined, most natural product you can find.

COCONUT SPREAD

A relatively new product that we find works well in some pie crusts and baked goods. It's also delicious spread on toast.

MILK SUBSTITUTES

Almond milk is one of the newest stars in this category. Its mild flavor and rich body mean it stands in well anywhere a thicker, richer milk product is needed. **Soymilk**, either sweetened, unsweetened, or vanilla-flavored, is something we're rarely without. We use it for everything from lightening soups to making smoothies. Rice milk and the newer refrigerated coconut milk in cartons also work well. Test them out and see which ones work best with your personal taste and dietary preferences.

ENER-G EGG REPLACER

This vegan, gluten-free egg substitute has been a lifesaver for baking (but only baking: try to scramble it and you'll be in trouble!). Made from tapioca and potato starches plus natural leavening agents, this powder really does effectively replace eggs when diluted with water. It'll give lift to your muffins, lightness to cakes and pastries—even add some levity to savory casseroles.

ALL NATURAL IMITATION CHICKEN OR BEEF SEASONING

We look for the natural versions with as short an ingredient list as possible. They get used in soups, stews, sauces, and stir-fries.

VEGAN MAYONNAISE (VEGENAISE)

One taste and you're hooked: This egg-free mayo substitute tastes as good as, or better than, old-fashioned mayo.

ORGANIC NON-GMO SILKEN TOFU

Look for the extra-soft silken tofu (we like Mori-Nu brand, which comes in a twelve-ounce, shelf-stable box). It stands in for eggs in batters, adds silkiness and body to desserts puddings and custards, and helps replace protein in meals.

ORGANIC, NON-GMO FIRM TOFU

A wonderful product that, when cooked properly, can add character to a recipe as opposed to just taking up space. We like it dry-fried, as we do in our Broccoli Pad Thai (recipe page 47), but you can also just throw it into any stir-fry or soup.

EARTH BALANCE BUTTERY STICKS

Made with non-GMO, expeller-pressed oil and no trans-fats, this is margarine you can feel pretty good about. The buttery sticks do the trick for desserts, helping us make great pie crusts and flaky cookies.

VEGAN WORCESTERSHIRE SAUCE (RECIPE PAGE 184)

We don't eat fish, so we came up with this animal-free version of the English classic. It strikes the same perfect balance of sweet, spicy, and tangy—making it a great addition to a variety of dishes. An added bonus: If stored properly, it'll last a very long time in your fridge.

NO-FISH FISH SAUCE (RECIPE PAGE 179)

Fish sauce without fish? We didn't think so either, but then tried versions that use seaweed and mushrooms to duplicate the mouthwatering *umami* that comes naturally from the Southeast Asian original. Splash into salads, or use in curries, soups, and dipping sauces. This is our easy-to-make version.

SOY SOUR CREAM
(RECIPE PAGE 180)

Lecithin and Instant Clear Jel help give this nondairy sour cream body. Its silky texture makes it a great base for dips, topping for desserts, and binder for casseroles.

INSTANT CLEAR JEL

A derivative of cornstarch that can withstand higher temperatures, dissolves quickly, and serves as a binder in jellies, jams, and other products. Find it in your local health food store or online.

LIQUID LECITHIN

Since we don't use eggs, this non-GMO, soy-derived product helps replace them in baked goods. Liquid lecithin helps doughs lighten and rise and synthesizes ingredients. Find it in your local health food store or online.

NUTRITIONAL YEAST

This flaky strain of yeast should be a staple in every kitchen; not only is it a reliable source of vitamin B_{12} and other relatives in the B complex, its unique flavor mimics that of cheese in many recipes. Try a shake or two of it on popcorn and you'll be converted, too.

SUCANAT

Unlike regular processed sugar, which has been stripped of its molasses, Sucanat contains molasses, which explains its dark brown color and slightly moist consistency. We like its flavor in place of brown sugar in desserts, sauces, and other dishes.

EVAPORATED CANE JUICE CRYSTALS

We've got nothing against plain white sugar, but if you can find it (and your budget allows), try to use evaporated cane juice crystals. Their main advantage over white sugar is that they're less processed, which explains their slightly darker color—some of the original molasses remains in the finished product. Use it in place of sugar anywhere, but by all means use regular sugar if that's what you can find.

Recipes

Apple Fritters

Makes 10 to 12 fritters

We affectionately call these crispy, free-form doughnuts our "air fare" fritters. Every year, my sister makes and sells them to pay for her journey to visit us for the May garden show in Mansfield. Once you taste them, you'll see why they get her where she needs to go. Try to make irregular shapes with lots of points, holes, and fingers, which will make the fritters crunchier. We've lightened the glaze by reducing the sugar and adding a little lemon juice into the mix to cut the recipe's richness.

Fritters
Vegetable oil for frying
2 cups bread flour
2 cups finely chopped Granny Smith
    apples
1 cup warm water
1 packet (2¼ teaspoons)
    active dry yeast
⅓ cup evaporated cane juice
    crystals
¾ teaspoon salt

Glaze
1½ cups confectioner's sugar
4 teaspoons lemon juice
1 tablespoon water or soymilk

Preheat 4 inches of oil to 350°F in a deep fryer or a large Dutch oven. Combine flour, apples, water, yeast, cane juice crystals, and salt in a large bowl and stir until a sticky batter forms. Drop batter by the quarter cupful into hot oil and fry, turning once, until golden brown and crispy, 2 to 3 minutes. While fritters are still warm, whisk together the sugar, lemon juice, and water until smooth and pour half the glaze over fritters. Let glaze harden, then turn and pour remaining glaze over bottom side of fritters.

Pink Pearl Applesauce

Makes 4½ cups

When we settled in Montana, we didn't have any apple orchards, but we could always count on our grandparents Opal and Lowell in Wenatchee, Washington, to help us get our fill. The best of the bunch were sold, but we happily gleaned the seconds to make tart, fresh apple cider. I'd collect Granny Smiths and put them through the cider press, barely able to wait to take the first sip from the metal cups I held out under the press. When in Washington, Mom would also make the most amazing applesauce using Macintosh apples, whose skins would turn the sauce pink before it passed through the food mill. Here, we use Pink Pearls, an incredible heirloom with a very short growing season but the most intense rosy flesh. Don't worry—if you can't find Pink Pearls, use Macintoshes—cook them with the skins on and pass through a food mill to complete the process.

12 Pink Pearl or 8 Macintosh apples
(3½ pounds), cored and sliced (about 10 cups)

½ cup water
½ cup agave nectar
1 tablespoon lemon juice

Place apples and water in a saucepan and bring to a boil; apples will release more liquid. Reduce heat to a simmer and cook, stirring, until apples disintegrate and mixture thickens, 12 to 15 minutes. Stir in agave nectar and lemon juice and simmer an additional 5 to 10 minutes. Remove from heat and cool; pass through a food mill and discard solids.

Applesauce will keep in refrigerator for up to 1 week; stir to incorporate any separated liquid before serving.

Apple-Raisin Samosas

Makes 32 samosas

I love flavors from all over the world, and samosas—those little stuffed packets from India—take kindly to a lot of different fillings, both sweet and savory. Here, we came up with an apple-and-raisin version that works especially well with firm heirlooms such as Gravensteins or Northern Spies, which maintain their bite even after a quick, hot fry.

Dough
1¾ cups all-purpose flour, plus more for kneading
1 teaspoon salt
1 tablespoon coconut oil, barely melted
½ cup ice water, plus more if necessary

Filling
2 tablespoons vegetable oil
1 small onion, diced (1 cup)
1 teaspoon garam masala seasoning
(available at specialty and Indian markets and at *www.penzeys.com*)
¼ teaspoon mustard seeds
¼ teaspoon chili flakes
1 tablespoon freshly grated ginger
2 cloves minced garlic
2 large apples, peeled and finely diced (about 3 cups)
⅓ cup golden raisins
½ teaspoon salt
½ teaspoon freshly ground black pepper
Vegetable oil for frying

Make dough:
Combine flour and salt in a medium bowl. Add the oil and rub the mixture with your fingers until evenly incorporated into flour. Add the water and stir with a wooden spoon until a sticky dough forms. Turn dough out onto a lightly floured surface and knead until smooth, 4 to 5 minutes. Transfer to a lightly oiled bowl, cover with a warm towel, and rest for 30 minutes. While dough is resting, make filling.

Make filling:
Heat oil in a heavy skillet over medium heat. Add onions and cook, stirring, for 2 minutes. Add garam masala, mustard seeds, and chili flakes and cook until onions are soft and translucent, an additional 5 to 6 minutes. Add ginger and garlic and cook an additional 2 minutes. Stir in apples, raisins, salt, and pepper, and cook an additional minute (don't cook too long—you don't want the apples to get too soft). Remove from flame and cool slightly.

Make samosas:

Knead dough slightly. Divide into two equal-sized balls, roll each ball out into a long, thin rope (about ½ inch thick), and refrigerate an additional 15 minutes. Cut each rope into 8 equal-sized pieces. Roll each piece into a smooth circle and then into a thin 6-inch disc using a rolling pin. Cut each disc in half. To form cones out of the dough, moisten the top edge of one semicircle with water, then fold the semicircle in half, pinching the joined straight edges to form a tight seam and a pouch. Hold the pouch in your hand and carefully fill each half with about 1 tablespoon filling. Moisten edges and fold over to crimp into a samosa-shaped triangle. Repeat.

Heat 2 inches of oil in a cast-iron skillet to 350°F. Fry samosas a few at a time until puffy, golden, and crisp, 2 to 3 minutes total. Drain on paper towels and serve with the condiment of your choice.

Heirloom Apple Pie

Serves 8 to 10

This recipe, developed by my sister, always gets rave reviews. This two-crust pie works best with tart apples like Granny Smith and Northern Spies, or even the rich, lush taste of the lumpy, but no less delicious, Calville Blanc, known as the be-all and end-all of apple-pie apples. We make our crust using coconut oil, a new favorite in the vegan kitchen. It makes an incredibly light crust that's as ethereally flaky as any we've seen or tasted. A word to the uninitiated: Coconut oil is incredibly temperature-sensitive. At room temperature it's solid and opaque, but at the first sight of heat it melts, and a flash of cold makes it rock-hard. You may have to experiment a bit depending on the temperature of your home and equipment, but we think you'll find the trial and error worthwhile. The addition of a bit of coconut cream stabilizes this dough; if you want to use all coconut oil, prepare to do a bit of patching here and there.

Pie Crust

2 cups unbleached all-purpose flour

¾ teaspoon salt

1 tablespoon evaporated cane juice crystals

⅔ cup coconut oil, solid at room temperature

2 tablespoons solid coconut cream, from the top of a can of coconut milk

¼ cup ice water

Pie Filling

8½–9 cups tart heirloom apples, peeled, quartered, and sliced (about 3½ pounds)

¾ cup evaporated cane juice crystals

¼ cup unbleached all-purpose flour

¾ teaspoon salt

½ teaspoon cinnamon

Coarse sanding sugar for dusting pie

Pulse flour, salt, and cane juice crystals in a food processor five times. Add coconut oil and coconut cream and pulse until pea-sized lumps form. Add water and continue to pulse until a ball forms, 15 to 20 pulses, being careful not to overwork. Divide dough into 2 pieces and form into two 4-inch discs, trying to make the edges as smooth as possible (this makes for a more uniform disc when rolling out). Wrap each disc and chill until dough is firmer but not hard, 15 to 20 minutes. While dough is chilling, toss apples, cane juice crystals, flour, salt, and cinnamon in a bowl. Let rest until juices begin to form; reserve.

Arrange rack in center of oven and preheat to 425°F. Spray a 9-inch pie plate with cooking spray; reserve.

Remove one dough disc from refrigerator. Place between 2 layers of wax paper. With a rolling pin, gently roll into a 12-inch circle. Return to refrigerator to chill for 3 to 4 minutes.

Gently lift top layer of wax paper, then fit dough into prepared pie plate. Pour apple mixture into pie plate, then remove second dough from refrigerator and roll out using same method used for bottom crust. Remove top layer of wax paper, and drape pie dough over apple mixture. Pinch edges of dough together, then tuck overhang under itself so pie dough rests on edge of plate. Using a fork, crimp edge decoratively. Sprinkle top lightly with sanding sugar. Using a knife or cookie cutter, make several inch-long slashes on top of pie dough. Using thin strips of foil or crust protectors, line edges of pie to prevent burning.

Place pie on a foil-lined, rimmed baking sheet and bake for 25 to 30 minutes (pie should still be light in color).

Reduce heat to 350°F and bake until filling is bubbly, apples are soft, and top is browned, an additional 50 to 60 minutes. Remove from oven and cool before serving.

Preserved Spiced Apricots

Makes 4 quarts

These apricots are processed using the cold-pack method, where raw fruit is covered in hot syrup and then processed in a water bath. Make sure to use unblemished, perfect fruit here. You won't notice the difference immediately, but once the fruit sits in the pantry for a few weeks, the quality begins to reveal itself. If it's blemished or bruised, the fruit will begin to darken and get mushy over time. If you don't like spice, simply omit the cinnamon and star anise.

6 cups water

1½ cups evaporated cane juice crystals

10 pounds ripe apricots, pitted, skins on

⅓ cup fresh lemon juice

4 cinnamon sticks, rinsed in hot water

4 star anise, rinsed in hot water

Combine water and cane juice crystals in a large saucepan. Bring to a boil, stirring to dissolve crystals, and reduce heat to a simmer; cover and keep hot.

Place apricots in a large bowl and toss gently with lemon juice. Place fruit into sterilized quart jars and add 1 cinnamon stick and 1 star anise to each jar. Pour hot syrup over fruit, leaving ½-inch headspace.

Cap and seal jars and process in a water-bath canner for 30 minutes. Remove from heat and cool completely before labeling. Check seal after 24 hours and let sit in pantry for at least 1 week to allow cinnamon and star anise flavors to meld.

Stewed Apricot Cobbler

Serves 10 to 12

Memories of apricots in my mom and dad's orchards abound. I loved them as a child, especially harvesting them at their peak, when their floral scent wafted through the fields. Mom would can quarts and quarts of apricots every year, and we'd feast on them throughout the winter. For this cobbler recipe, any ripe variety will do. If you don't have preserved apricots, use the ripest, juiciest fresh apricots you can find.

4 quarts Preserved Spiced Apricots
  (recipe page 28), or other canned
  apricots
1 cup unbleached all-purpose flour
1 cup evaporated cane juice crystals
2 teaspoons baking powder
1 teaspoon salt

1 cup coconut milk
½ cup coconut spread or vegan buttery
  stick, melted
Coconut Whipped Cream (recipe page
  176) for topping

Preheat oven to 350° F.

Drain apricots, reserving liquid for another use. Place apricots in a large saucepan and bring to a low boil; apricots will release additional liquid. Reduce heat and keep simmering over low heat.

While apricots are simmering, whisk flour, cane juice crystals, baking powder, salt, and coconut milk in a bowl until smooth.

Melt spread in a small saucepan and pour into a 9- by 13-inch glass baking dish. Pour batter over melted shortening, then spoon simmering fruit evenly over batter. Bake until topping is browned and fruit is bubbling, 60 to 70 minutes.

Serve warm or cold; top with Coconut Whipped Cream or ice cream, if desired.

Oven Roasted Artichokes, Lemon Wedges, and Bull's Blood Beets over Shredded Beet Greens

Serves 6

We tend to eat a lot of artichokes when we're wintering in California, working at our Seed Bank store in Petaluma. When in season, they're so prolific that they can be had on the cheap, allowing us to find new ways to prepare them every year. Here, we roast them to keep their texture and to avoid the waterlogged leaves and hearts that can result from careless steaming. I've also fallen in love with Bull's Blood beets in the past few years, and so have our catalog customers, who've taken to both the gorgeous pink-ringed beets and the delicious, edible, deep-red leaves. The leaves make a great basis for a salad, and instead of the usual sauté, we serve them raw, topped with the gorgeous roasted artichokes, beets, and lemon wedges.

4 small Bull's Blood beets, leaves intact (about 1 pound)

4 medium artichokes (about 1½ pounds)

2 lemons, cut into thick wedges

¼ cup extra virgin olive oil, plus more for drizzling

4 whole cloves garlic

1 teaspoon sea salt, plus more for seasoning

½ teaspoon freshly ground black pepper

2 sprigs thyme

½ cup vegetable broth or water

Preheat oven to 400°F.

Trim leaves from beets and reserve. Scrub and dry beets, then wrap each beet individually in foil; place on a baking sheet and roast until tender-firm, about 1 hour. Remove from oven and cool in foil.

Trim ends off of beet leaves, then wash and dry leaves thoroughly. Pull leaves from stalks and chop roughly; store in a covered bowl in refrigerator until ready to use.

Remove outer leaves from artichokes. Cut off and discard top ½ inch of artichokes with a sharp knife, then snip off any remaining thorns with scissors. Trim bottom end of artichokes so that 1 inch of stem remains, then trim tough outer layer with a knife or vegetable peeler.

Cut artichokes into quarters. Using a paring knife, cut out furry choke and discard. Run artichoke quarters under cold water; drain and pat dry with a clean kitchen towel.

Toss artichokes and lemon wedges with olive oil, garlic cloves, salt, pepper, and thyme and arrange, cut-side down, in a large glass roasting pan or baking dish. Add broth and cover with foil. Place artichokes in same oven as beets and roast until artichokes are almost tender, about 1 hour (beets can be removed before artichokes are done; some outer artichoke leaves will remain tough; discard them if inedible). Do not discard lemon wedges.

Remove beets from foil when cool enough to handle, slip off skins and slice each beet into 6 wedges.

Arrange beet leaves on a platter and top with roasted artichokes, beet wedges, and lemon wedges.

Drizzle with olive oil and salt, and let people squeeze roasted lemon wedges over the salad after serving themselves.

Shaved Asparagus and Arugula Salad with Coconut-Lime Dressing

Makes 6 cups

Asparagus is a family favorite that we buy by the boxful at our local Amish produce auction. Since it's one of the first veggies on the table in the spring, we might be up against a handful of excited bidders also looking to put this nutritious spring treat on their own tables. Thankfully, we win as much as we lose, allowing us to make dishes like this crunchy raw salad, which lets the nuttier side of asparagus shine through. You can use what's available at your local grocer or farmers' market (consider blush-budded Precoce D'Argenteuil) or, if you live in an area where asparagus grows wild, use foraged spears for this recipe.

½ pound asparagus stalks, trimmed

4 cups arugula

½ pint multicolored heirloom cherry tomatoes, halved

¼ cup coconut milk

2 tablespoons lime juice

1 teaspoon lime zest

1 teaspoon agave nectar

¼ teaspoon salt

Using a sharp vegetable peeler, shave asparagus into thin ribbons and reserve. Arrange arugula leaves on a platter and top with asparagus ribbons and tomatoes. Whisk together coconut milk, lime juice and zest, agave nectar, and salt and drizzle on top of salad.

Asparagus and Shiitake Stir-Fry with Peanut Sauce

Serves 4

Throughout the winter months, we wait with great anticipation for the first homegrown vegetable to make its debut. Asparagus is often the first sign of freshly harvested produce in our kitchen, and we love the way its crisp, springlike flavor pairs with a nutty peanut sauce in this spring dish. We like to use dark blue agave nectar in this recipe, but feel free to substitute regular agave nectar, brown sugar, or Sucanat.

Peanut Sauce (makes 1¼ cup)
½ cup natural creamy peanut butter
5 tablespoons seasoned rice vinegar
5 tablespoons blue agave nectar
3 tablespoons soy sauce
3 cloves chopped fresh garlic
1 tablespoon minced ginger
2 teaspoons chili paste, or more to taste
1 tablespoon sesame oil

Stir-Fry
2 tablespoons canola oil
¼ cup thinly sliced shallots
2 cloves garlic, thinly sliced
1 pound asparagus spears, ends trimmed, spears chopped into 2-inch pieces
1 red bell pepper, seeded and cut into thin strips
8 ounces shiitake mushrooms, stems removed, thinly sliced
¼ cup water, plus more to taste
Cooked jasmine rice

Make sauce:
Combine all ingredients together in a small saucepan and whisk until smooth. Bring to a boil, reduce heat, and simmer until sauce thickens slightly, 2 to 3 minutes. Remove from heat and cool. Sauce will keep, refrigerated, in an airtight container for up to 10 days.

Make stir-fry:
Heat oil in a large, heavy skillet or wok over medium-high heat until hot but not smoking. Add shallots and garlic and cook,

stirring, until fragrant and shallots are softened, 2 to 3 minutes. Add asparagus, peppers, mushrooms, and water and cook over medium-high heat until mushrooms are softened and asparagus and peppers are tender-crisp, an additional 2 to 3 minutes, adding more water by the tablespoonful if vegetables become too dry.

Add peanut sauce and cook until sauce is absorbed and thickened, 1 to 2 minutes. Serve with rice.

Vegetable Tempura with Thai Basil

Serves 8

Emilee and I love food history, and we're always reading up on dishes and their origins. Portuguese Catholic missionaries brought tempura to Japan in the sixteenth century. Traditionally, Catholics served this dish as a vegetarian option during Lent and other times when they abstained from eating meat. At the Baker Creek restaurant, we are always on our toes come "tempura day," as this is one of the most popular dishes we serve to employees and guests alike. The Thai basil leaves give the batter just a hint of intrigue that's pleasing, but mysteriously hard to identify.

Vegetable oil for frying
2½ cups unbleached all-purpose flour
2 cups ice-cold seltzer water or club soda
1 tablespoon plus one teaspoon baking
   powder
8 Thai basil leaves
1 teaspoon paprika

1 teaspoon salt, plus more for seasoning
3 cups broccoli florets, very lightly steamed
3 cups cauliflower florets, very lightly
   steamed
1 medium onion, sliced into rings
1 medium garnet yam, peeled and thinly
   sliced

Heat 5 inches of oil in a large pot to 350° or fill a deep-fryer according to manufacturer's instructions. Combine flour, seltzer, baking powder, basil, paprika, and salt in a blender and puree until smooth, 15 to 20 seconds (mixture will resemble thick pancake batter). Transfer to a bowl. When the oil is hot, use tongs to dip each vegetable into the batter and place in the heated oil a few pieces at a time. Remove vegetables once they float to the surface and are a light golden brown, 2 to 3 minutes total. Drain on paper towels, sprinkle with salt, and serve with Sweet Thai Chili Sauce (recipe page 181) or the Peanut Sauce used in our Asparagus and Shiitake Stir-Fry (recipe page 33).

Pickled Chili-Garlic Green Beans

Makes 5 pints

I like beans when they still taste like a vegetable, and short of lightly steaming them, pickling is a great way to keep them crisp and perky. This is a basic pickling liquid, but you can adjust the amount of spice to your liking. It's fun to use different varieties of beans; consider combining Buerre de Rocquencourt and Tongue varieties for a lovely contrast.

3½ cups white vinegar
3½ cups water
6 tablespoons kosher salt
1 tablespoon sugar
½ teaspoon chili flakes

5 garlic cloves
2½ teaspoons black peppercorns
5 sprigs dill
3 pounds green beans, washed, trimmed, and cut into 2-inch pieces

Bring vinegar, water, salt, sugar, and chili flakes to a boil. Reduce heat and simmer vigorously.

Place 1 garlic clove, ½ teaspoon peppercorns, and a dill sprig in each of 5 hot, sterilized pint-sized jars.

Tightly pack green beans into jars, then pour hot pickling liquid over them, making sure green beans are covered in liquid but leaving ½ inch of space at the top of each jar.

Seal tightly and process in a hot water bath for 10 minutes.

Cool completely before labeling, check seal after 24 hours, and let flavors marry for 2 to 3 weeks before opening and serving.

Edamame Hummus

Makes about 4 cups

Edamame has become such a part of regular dining in America, but what many people don't realize is that edamame are humble soybeans! I've always disliked dried beans (shhhh! I know many find them indispensible); I prefer mine fresh. You can purchase edamame at a local farmers' market and shell the beans yourself, but they also come frozen in the super-market, pre-shelled and ready to use in a million ways. Here, they replace chickpeas in hum-mus, and they lend a nice green color and interesting texture to an otherwise familar recipe. We add our own homemade tahini, plus some silken tofu for creaminess and body. You may like it so much that you never go back to the original version.

1 16-ounce bag frozen shelled edamame, or 2½ cups fresh shelled edamame

1 garlic clove

3 tablespoons fresh lemon juice

¼ cup olive oil, plus more for drizzling

2 tablespoons Homemade Tahini (recipe page 178)

8 ounces soft silken tofu

1 teaspoon salt

½ teaspoon freshly ground black pepper

⅛ teaspoon cayenne pepper

Paprika for garnish

Bring 6 cups of water to a boil. Add edamame and let water come back to a boil.

Cook until very soft, 15 to 20 minutes. Drain, reserving ¾ cup of the cooking liquid.

Reserve 1 tablespoon edamame for garnish. Transfer edamame to a blender, then add the remaining ingredients except for the paprika with ½ cup of the cooking liquid and blend until smooth, adding more of the liquid if necessary. Season with additional salt and pepper to taste.

Transfer puree to a serving bowl. Drizzle with olive oil and sprinkle with paprika. Garnish with reserved edamame.

Szechuan Green Beans

Makes 4 cups

These delicious stir-fried beans are an adaptation of the ones you find in Chinese restaurants. They can be made with everything from haricots verts, Purple Royalty Pod Bush Beans, or even our Chinese Long Beans, which measure up to a whopping foot and a half long and boast a distinctive, nutty flavor. Growers recommend harvesting them at about eighteen inches—the longer they grow, the tougher they get. The tamarind-laced sauce is great on all kinds of sautéed vegetables and Asian dishes.

Tamarind Sauce
3 tablespoons soy sauce

3 tablespoons water

2 tablespoons Sweet Thai Chili Sauce (recipe page 181)

1 tablespoon tamarind paste

1 teaspoon chili flakes

Green Beans
3 tablespoons canola oil, divided

1 pound (2½ to 3 cups) green beans, trimmed (if using Chinese long beans, trim beans to 3 to 4 inches in length)

½ cup thinly sliced onions

5 cloves minced garlic

2 tablespoon minced ginger

Cooked jasmine rice

Make tamarind sauce:

Combine soy sauce, water, chili sauce, tamarind paste, and chili flakes in a bowl and reserve.

Make beans:

Heat 1 tablespoon oil in a large wok or skillet over high heat until very hot but not smoking. Add beans and cook, tossing occasionally, until they are charred and slightly shriveled, 5 to 6 minutes. Remove from pan and reserve.

Add remaining 2 tablespoons oil and cook onions until translucent, 2 minutes. Add garlic and ginger and cook an additional 2 minutes. Return green beans to pan, pour sauce over vegetables, and cook until the sauce slightly thickens and coats the beans, 1 to 2 minutes (add additional tablespoons of water if sauce thickens too much).

Serve over rice.

Grilled Beets

Serves 4 to 6

Most people don't think of the grill for beets, but these brightly colored discs maintain their color over the fire, and the charred grill marks make for a beautiful plate. The caramelization that forms on the edges of the beets only adds to their great flavor. The accompanying Green Goddess Dressing is a family favorite. Its secret thickening ingredient is cashews, which add a silky creaminess with no dairy products. It works as well as a dip with cut-up vegetables or a sandwich spread as it does on salad and cooked vegetables. It's also a great way to use up whichever herbs you happen to have lying around the house or overflowing in the garden on any given day. To make the dressing even thicker, add an additional ¼ cup cashews to the recipe. If you desire a thinner consistency, add a bit more water or lemon juice.

1½ pounds red and yellow beets
2 tablespoons olive oil

1 teaspoon salt, divided
½ teaspoon pepper, divided

Preheat a grill or grill pan over medium-high heat. Peel and slice beets into ¼-inch slices, keeping peeled red and yellow beets separate so the red ones don't stain the yellow ones.

Toss yellow beets, 1 tablespoon olive oil, ½ teaspoon salt, and ¼ teaspoon pepper in a bowl. Place on grill, then toss red beets with remaining olive oil, salt, and pepper. Place red beets on grill. Grill until grill marks form on underside, 5 to 6 minutes. Flip and grill until cooked through, an additional 4 to 5 minutes. Transfer to a plate and cover with foil to keep warm. Serve with Green Goddess Dressing (recipe page 40).

Green Goddess Dressing

Makes 2 cups

½ cup water

⅓ cup fresh lemon juice

⅓ cup raw cashews

2 crushed garlic cloves

1 teaspoon salt

¼ teaspoon freshly ground pepper

1 cup assorted fresh herbs, such as basil, mint, tarragon, cilantro, and parsley

¾ cup olive oil

2 tablespoons nutritional yeast

Puree water, lemon juice, cashews, garlic, salt, and pepper in a blender until very smooth, 30 seconds. Add herbs and blend until puree is smooth and green, an additional 30 seconds. With blender running, drizzle olive oil in a small stream until dressing is thick and smooth, then add nutritional yeast and blend an additional 5 seconds. Transfer to an airtight container and chill (dressing will thicken as it chills). Serve with Grilled Beets (recipe page 39). Dressing will keep, covered in an airtight container, in refrigerator for up to 1 week.

Watermelon Radish and Yellow Beet Salad with Lemon and Mint Oil Dressing

Serves 6

The watermelon radish, with its fuchsia starburst pattern and crisp radish flavor, is one of the most showstopping vegetables in the Baker Creek Heirloom Seed catalog. Contrasting it with yellow beets and a light, lemony mint dressing makes for a perfect, no-fuss summertime salad. Use other gorgeous radishes, like Chinese Red Meat, if you can't find the watermelon variety.

Mint Oil Dressing (makes 1 cup)
2 cups fresh mint, plus more for garnish
1 cup mild extra-virgin olive oil
⅓ cup lemon juice
1 teaspoon finely grated lemon zest
½ teaspoon salt

Salad
1 medium yellow beet (4 ounces), peeled
1 medium watermelon radish (4 ounces), peeled

Make dressing:

Prepare an ice water bath in a medium-sized bowl. Bring a small pot of water to a boil and blanch mint for 5 seconds. Remove to ice bath for 30 seconds, then wring out excess moisture from mint and transfer to a blender. Add olive oil and blend on high for 1 minute. Strain oil from solids into a bowl; discard solids. Add lemon juice, zest, and salt and whisk; reserve.

Make salad:

Using a mandolin slicer or a very sharp knife, slice paper-thin slices of the beets and radishes. Arrange 5 slices of each vegetable in alternating order on each of 6 plates and drizzle each plate with 1 tablespoon dressing (additional dressing will remain). Garnish with additional mint leaves.

Blackberry-Raspberry Oatmeal Bars

Makes 24 bars

We used to go to the mountains to pick wild blackberries and huckleberries. Sometimes, you just knew there were bears nearby. I never came face-to-face with one, but I can remember hearing them rustling their way through the bushes within earshot. It made the hairs on my neck stand right up on end—and made for some vivid campfire stories. These days, we've got berries on our Baker Creek farm, but no bears—a good thing, too, since our little daughter, Sasha, has never met a berry she didn't love . . . especially one she picks herself.

⅓ cup coconut oil

½ cup vegan buttery stick

¾ cup evaporated cane juice crystals

½ cup Sucanat crystals or brown sugar

¾ cup unbleached all-purpose flour

¾ cup whole wheat pastry flour

1½ cups old-fashioned rolled oats

1½ teaspoons baking powder

½ teaspoon salt

1 cup **Blackberry Jam** (recipe page 43)

1 cup fresh raspberries

Cream coconut oil, margarine, cane juice crystals, and Sucanat crystals in a stand mixer until light and fluffy, 1 to 2 minutes.

Sift flours, oats, baking powder, and salt and add to mixture in 2 parts, scraping down sides of mixer to incorporate dry ingredients if necessary; dough will be loose.

Press ⅔ of the dough into the bottom of a small jelly roll pan or quarter-sheet pan (about 8 x 12 inches).

Combine jam and berries in a bowl, stirring to break up fresh berries. Spread over dough using an offset spatula. Sprinkle remaining dough evenly over filling and bake until lightly browned and set, about 1 hour.

Cool and cut into 24 bars.

Blackberry Jam

Makes 4 pint jars

Our daughter, Sasha, perks up when she hears the call for berry picking around our house. She eagerly grabs her little bucket and is the first one out the door to help my dad pick black-berries by the handful. My mom sells her blackberry jam in the bakery on our farm—many make a special trip just to get some.

  8 cups ripe blackberries
  7 cups evaporated cane juice crystals
  2½ tablespoons lemon juice

Place blackberries in a large saucepan 2 cups at a time, crushing berries after each addition.

Add cane juice crystals and lemon juice, bring to a boil and cook, stirring, until bubbly, 4 to 5 minutes.

Reduce heat to medium and cook until thickened slightly, skimming foam, 25 to 30 minutes.

Remove from heat and pour into sterilized pint jars. Cap and seal jars, then process in a water bath canner for 15 minutes. Remove from heat and cool completely before labeling. Check seals before storing.

Blueberry Pancakes

Makes 8 large pancakes

When you grow up on a farm, berries aren't something you buy in a clamshell container from an air-conditioned supermarket aisle—they're a seasonal treasure that you come to expect as a warm-weather rite of passage. Every summer in my early childhood years, before we moved to Missouri, we'd pick bushels and bushels in my parents' garden and among the wilderness areas of the northwestern United States. There were almost too many to get to! My mom would put up jars of berry jam for the wintertime, and somewhere there are incriminating pictures of me, fingers and mouth stained with the blue juice of pure childhood bliss.

Soy Buttermilk
2 cups soymilk
1 tablespoon fresh lemon juice

Pancakes
2 cups all-purpose unbleached flour
2 tablespoons sugar
2 teaspoons baking powder
½ teaspoon baking soda
½ teaspoon sea salt
4 tablespoons Ener-G egg replacer powder (not diluted)
3 tablespoons melted coconut oil, plus more for cooking pancakes
1½ cups blueberries, plus more for serving
Maple syrup for serving

Make soy buttermilk:
Warm soymilk slightly in a small saucepan, add lemon juice, stir, and remove from heat; let thicken at least 30 minutes or up to 2 hours at room temperature.

Make pancakes:
Whisk dry ingredients in a large bowl, add coconut oil and Soy Buttermilk and whisk until just incorporated. Do not overmix; some small flour lumps are okay.

Heat a cast-iron skillet over medium heat until hot and brush with additional coconut oil. Pour batter into skillet by the ½ cupful, then sprinkle with 2 to 3 tablespoons blueberries. Cook until bubbles form in center of pancakes and edges are browned, 1 to 2 minutes, then flip and cook until browned on other side, an additional 1 to 2 minutes. Cook additional pancakes and serve with additional berries, maple syrup, or Spiced Blackberry Syrup (recipe page 45).

Spiced Blackberry Syrup

Makes 1 cup

In my estimation, blackberry syrup drizzled over pancakes, waffles, or ice cream is the ideal dessert. It's almost laughably easy, so I added some interesting spices to give the syrup an edge. Interchange what you like for the spices here or leave them out altogether. Just make sure to use the ripest, juiciest, sun-kissed blackberries you can find.

4 cups blackberries (about 1¼ pounds)
¾ cup water
1 cup evaporated cane juice crystals or
    light agave nectar

1 bay leaf
10 peppercorns
2 cardamom pods
1 cinnamon stick

Combine all ingredients in a saucepan and bring to a boil. Reduce heat and simmer for 30 minutes, stirring and mashing fruit. Remove from heat and strain through a fine-meshed sieve, pushing down on solids to release as much liquid as possible. Discard solids. Syrup can be refrigerated in an airtight container for up to 1 month.

Strawberry Ice Cream

Makes 4 cups

During strawberry season, Mom made so many pies it got to the point where we'd be begging for a break. I can't say I ever feel the same way anymore, but we also use juicy summer berries to make this blender ice cream. Silken tofu gives it body and a dairy-like richness without the lactose.

1 12-ounce package firm silken tofu
1¼ cups evaporated cane juice crystals
¾ cup canola oil
½ cup plain soymilk
3 tablespoons lemon juice
2 teaspoons vanilla extract

¼ teaspoon salt
¾ pound fresh strawberries, rinsed,
  hulled, and sliced (about 2½ cups), plus
  more for serving
2 teaspoons lemon zest
Mint leaves for garnish

Place tofu, cane juice crystals, oil, soymilk, lemon juice, vanilla, and salt in a blender and blend until smooth, 30 seconds.

Add strawberries and zest and pulse until berries are incorporated but not completely smooth, 15 pulses. Place in a bowl, cover, and refrigerate for 4 hours or up to 24.

Freeze in ice cream maker according to manufacturer's instructions. Serve garnished with fresh strawberries and mint leaves.

Broccoli Pad Thai

Serves 3 to 4

There aren't many Asian restaurants in our area, and Emilee didn't have a lot of exposure to my favorite cuisine when we met. Her first encounter with Thai food actually happened when I took her out for dinner in St. Louis on one of our first dates. As she tells it, she was nervous about a lot of things, our date and trying a new cuisine high among them. I kept things simple by ordering two plates of pad thai, reassuring Emilee that everyone who tries it, likes it. While we waited for the order to arrive, I shared story after story of my trips through Thailand and the sights, sounds, and flavors of the country that I had grown to love so much. Needless to say, she loved the dish and it's now one of her favorites, too. Every time we eat it, she says she's reminded of her encounter with pad thai . . . with a side of butterflies.

> *In the 1930s and 1940s, cooking pad thai was encouraged in Thailand, as rice exports were essential to the Thai economy. Rice noodles became a welcomed solution for the economy and the Thai kitchen.*

Sauce
½ cup water
4 tablespoons tamarind concentrate
5 tablespoons Sucanat or brown sugar
3 tablespoons soy sauce
2 tablespoons No-Fish Fish Sauce (recipe page 179)
1 teaspoon Sriracha or chili-garlic sauce

Pad Thai
6 ounces dried rice sticks (Thai rice noodles for pad thai)
Sesame oil for coating noodles

1 14.5-ounce package extra-firm tofu, halved lengthwise and cut into ¼-inch-thick rectangles
½ teaspoon salt
½ teaspoon freshly ground black pepper
2 tablespoons canola oil
4 shallots, thinly sliced (about 1¼ cups)
4 cloves minced garlic
1 cup (4 ounces) Napa cabbage, shredded
2 cups small broccoli florets
1½ cups (about 4 ounces) bean sprouts
2 tablespoons chopped roasted peanuts
2 limes, cut into wedges

Make sauce:

Whisk together water, tamarind, Sucanat, soy sauce, Fish Sauce, and Sriracha sauce; reserve.

Make pad thai:

Place rice noodles in a large bowl and cover with hot water. Allow to soak until tender, 9 to 10 minutes. Drain and toss with sesame oil to prevent sticking.

While noodles are soaking, sprinkle tofu with salt and pepper and arrange in a single layer in a very large (12-inch) nonstick skillet (or work in smaller batches) with no oil or cooking spray. Heat tofu over high heat, pressing every minute or two to release liquid, about 4 minutes per side. Remove from pan, slice into strips, and reserve.

In a large wok or skillet, heat oil over medium heat. Sauté shallots until translucent, 5 to 6 minutes. Add garlic and cook an additional minute. Add cabbage and broccoli and cook until tender-crisp, 3 to 4 minutes. Add bean sprouts, noodles, tofu, and reserved sauce. Toss, and cook until noodles are coated and sauce is absorbed, an additional 2 to 3 minutes.

Serve with chopped peanuts and lime wedges.

Broccoli Potstickers

Makes about 25 potstickers

Potstickers are one of those dishes that seem so complicated at the Chinese restaurant. In Mandarin Chinese they're translated as "pan stick" because of the way they cling dearly to the bottom of the skillet before they steam and release. The first time we made these, we were surprised at how easy the dough was—just plain old flour, hot water, and salt. We promise, there's no secret! We like to fill ours with broccoli and onions, but you could vary the filling as many ways as you can think of, adding different vegetables, seasonings, tofu—whatever you like. Try making them with broccoli rabe for a distinctively strong, nutty, and slightly bitter broccoli flavor.

Dough
1 cup unbleached all-purpose flour, plus more for kneading
½ cup very hot water
¼ teaspoon salt

Filling
3 tablespoons vegetable oil, divided
1 cup finely diced onion
1 tablespoon minced fresh ginger
2 teaspoons minced garlic
3 cups broccoli florets, finely chopped (about 3 cups after chopping)
1 tablespoon soy sauce, plus more for serving
2 teaspoons sesame oil
1 teaspoon chili-garlic sauce

Make dough:
Combine flour, water, and salt in a bowl and stir with a spoon until a very dry dough forms (add additional flour by the tablespoonful as necessary). Turn out onto a lightly floured work surface and knead until dough is smooth, firm, and not sticky, 4 to 5 minutes, adding additional flour as necessary. Wrap in plastic wrap and chill while making filling.

Make filling:
Heat 2 tablespoons oil in a large, heavy skillet over medium-high heat. Add onions and cook, stirring, until lightly browned, 9 to 10 minutes. Add ginger and garlic and cook, stirring, an additional 2 minutes. Add broccoli, soy sauce, sesame oil, and chili-garlic sauce and cook, stirring, until broccoli is tender-crisp, an additional 3 to 4 minutes. Let cool.

Make potstickers:

Remove dough from refrigerator and cut into 2 pieces. Roll each piece into a 6-inch rope. Using a sharp knife, cut each rope into 12 pieces. Lightly flour a clean, dry work surface and roll each piece of dough into a 3-inch circle. Spoon 1 tablespoon filling into center of each disc and fold over, pinching and pleating as you seal the potsticker shut. Heat remaining oil in a large, heavy skillet with a cover over medium-high heat. Arrange 12 potstickers in the pan and fry bottoms, not moving potstickers, 1 to 2 minutes. Pour ¼ cup water into skillet, quickly cover and steam, until water is evaporated and dough is cooked through, 7 to 8 minutes. Using a metal spatula, remove potstickers from skillet (bottoms should be crisp and browned). Repeat with remaining potstickers and serve with soy sauce.

Heirloom Broccoli and Potato Casserole

Serves 6

This is straight-up comfort food, with nutritious broccoli as the centerpiece. Broccoli may very well just be my favorite vegetable, and I'm always marveling at how we find new ways to use it for dinner. This casserole is great for church suppers, Sunday brunches, and everything in between. Make sure to just lightly steam the broccoli, giving it a fighting chance to retain some texture while it bakes in its bread-crumb topping.

1 large potato, peeled and cubed (about 2½ cups)

4 cups broccoli florets

1 tablespoon extra virgin olive oil

1½ cups diced onions

2 tablespoons minced garlic

1¼ cups light coconut milk

2 tablespoons nutritional yeast flakes

1 teaspoon chopped marjoram

1 teaspoon chopped fresh rosemary

1 teaspoon salt, divided

¾ teaspoon freshly ground black pepper, divided

½ teaspoon cornstarch

1 cup fresh vegan bread crumbs

2 tablespoons coconut oil, melted

Preheat oven to 350°F.

Place potatoes in a steamer and steam until almost tender, 15 minutes. Add broccoli during last 5 minutes of steaming and steam until tender-crisp; roughly chop broccoli and reserve with potatoes.

While vegetables are steaming, heat oil in a heavy skillet over medium-high heat. Add onions and cook until lightly browned, 9 to 10 minutes. Add garlic and cook, stirring, an additional minute; reserve.

Oil a 9-inch square casserole dish and transfer potatoes and broccoli to dish. In a large bowl, combine the onions and garlic with the coconut milk, yeast flakes, marjoram, rosemary, ½ teaspoon each salt and pepper, and cornstarch and pour over the vegetables. Toss bread crumbs with coconut oil and remaining salt and pepper, pour over vegetables, and bake until heated through, 30 to 35 minutes.

Serve warm.

Broccoli-Almond Green and White Gazpacho

Makes 4 cups

When people think of gazpacho, they usually think of a chunky, red, tomato-laced soup filled with onions, garlic, and spice that originated in the Andalusian region of Spain. This version is inspired by *ajo blanco*, a type of gazpacho that stars blanched almonds and olive oil streamed in slowly to form a rich soup. Garlic and sherry vinegar lend a bit of necessary sharpness and heat, and the broccoli lends some nice color, too. It's so well respected in Spain, it's sometimes called "royal salad."

3 cups broccoli florets, lightly steamed, 1 floret chopped and reserved for garnish

1½ cups unsweetened almond milk, divided

½ cup blanched almonds, plus 2 tablespoons toasted chopped almonds for garnish

1 slice stale vegan white bread, crusts removed, moistened with ½ cup cold water

2 tablespoons sherry vinegar

1 small garlic clove

¾ teaspoon salt

¼ teaspoon freshly ground black pepper

½ cup olive oil

Combine broccoli, 1 cup almond milk, blanched almonds, bread, vinegar, garlic, salt, and pepper in a blender or food processor and puree until smooth, 30 seconds. With machine on, add olive oil in a slow stream until a thick soup forms.

Chill in refrigerator for at least 1 hour. Remove from refrigerator and thin with reserved ½ cup almond milk if soup is too thick. Divide among 4 bowls and garnish with chopped broccoli and toasted almonds.

Maple Brussels Sprouts with Tempeh Bacon

Serves 4

You either love Brussels sprouts or you hate them, but even if it's the latter, these crispy, smoky, sweet, and salty morsels will convert you to the other side. Sometimes I find getting the ratio of crisp outside to perfectly cooked inside difficult, and quartering the sprouts does the trick. Tempeh "bacon," made with a fermented wheat protein, doesn't need to feel like the poor stepsibling to the "real thing"—I think it adds a distinctive personality all its own.

3 tablespoons vegetable oil

6 strips tempeh "bacon," crumbled

¾ pound Brussels sprouts, trimmed and quartered

½ teaspoon salt

½ teaspoon smoked paprika

¼ teaspoon freshly ground black pepper

1½ tablespoons maple syrup, preferably grade B

Preheat oven to 500°F. Heat oil in a cast-iron skillet over medium-high heat. Add tempeh bacon and cook, stirring, until crisp, 3 to 4 minutes.

Add Brussels sprouts, salt, paprika, and pepper, and cook, stirring, until sprouts begin to soften, about 2 minutes. Add maple syrup and stir, then transfer skillet to oven. Roast, stirring midway through, until sprouts are charred, 8 to 9 minutes. Serve immediately.

Shaved Brussels Sprout and Radicchio Salad with Toasted Walnuts

Makes 5 cups

This is our take on the *tricolore* salads you find all over Italy, but this one's only *due-colore*—two-colored. I love the way the purple and green vegetable ribbons contrast against one another, and shaving Brussels sprouts preserves many of their nutrients and reveals a surprisingly delicate flavor you don't always get when you cook them. People tend to automatically peel off the outer leaves of Brussels sprouts, but the outer leaves of lettuce and cabbage often have the most nutrition—and the nicest color. In this case, the deep-green outer leaves add color contrast when you thinly shave the sprouts.

½ pound Brussels sprouts

1 small or ½ large head radicchio (about 4 ounces)

2 tablespoons champagne vinegar

½ teaspoon Dijon mustard

½ teaspoon maple syrup

½ teaspoon salt

¼ teaspoon freshly ground black pepper

5 tablespoons walnut oil

½ cup toasted chopped walnuts

Using a mandolin slicer or a food processor, thinly shred the Brussels sprouts and radicchio; transfer to a large bowl.

Whisk together the vinegar, mustard, maple syrup, salt, and pepper in a medium-sized bowl. Slowly whisk in walnut oil until dressing is creamy and opaque. Toss with shaved Brussels sprouts and radicchio and sprinkle with toasted chopped walnuts.

Coleslaw

Makes 8 cups

I ate a ton of cabbage as a child, and as a result I'm super sentimental about it. My grandmas both served it a million and one ways, from as a steamed or fried side dish with soy sauce and garlic to stuffing for Kraut Burgers. Cabbage is a wonderful link in our food supply; when not much else is in season, you can count on its beauty and heartiness. It lasts for months and makes any garden it graces extra lively with its tableau of colors and ruffled, often flower-like tops.

1 cup apple cider vinegar

1 cup agave nectar

½ head green cabbage (1 pound), such as Coeur de Beouf, finely sliced (about 5 cups)

½ head red cabbage (1 pound), such as Mammoth Red Rock, finely sliced (about 5 cups)

2 large carrots, peeled and grated (1½ cups)

2 scallions, thinly sliced

1 tablespoon finely chopped red onion

2 tablespoons chopped fresh parsley, plus more for garnish

⅔ cup Vegenaise

4 teaspoons fresh lemon juice

½ teaspoon salt

¼ teaspoon freshly ground black pepper

Whisk together vinegar and agave nectar and toss with green and red cabbages in a large bowl. Let stand for 30 minutes, stir, then let stand an additional 30 minutes.

Transfer to a colander and drain well, squeezing out as much liquid as possible.

Add carrot, scallion, red onion, and parsley and toss with cabbage. Whisk together Vegenaise, lemon juice, salt, and pepper, add to bowl, and stir to incorporate. Cover and refrigerate at least 1 hour or up to 24 hours before serving.

Sauerkraut

Makes 12 cups

One of the most popular booths at our Heirloom Exposition was the "fermentation station" run by our food-obsessed friends over at BiteClub Eats. Every day crowds gathered to watch seasoned pros make "living" foods with "controlled spoilage" like sourdough starter, fermented soybeans, vinegar, and sauerkraut. You'll be surprised how easy it is to make this salty, pitch-perfect kraut, from a recipe we adapted from new friend Marley Alexander Peifer. Just follow the steps closely, build in a healthy dose of patience, and reap the rewards every time you pile some on a sandwich or lunch plate.

5 pounds green cabbage, quartered, cored, and shredded

3 tablespoons salt

3 large carrots (1½ pounds), coarsely grated

1 tablespoon chopped ginger

2 cloves chopped garlic

Combine cabbage and salt in a large mixing bowl, mixing and squeezing with hands to help cabbage absorb salt; let rest for 1 hour.

Add carrots, ginger, and garlic to cabbage and mix thoroughly.

Transfer to a food-grade tub (available at restaurant-supply stores), foodsafe container, or fermentation crock.

Using clean hands, press cabbage mixture down, allowing juice to emerge from cabbage and cover the mixture (if liquid does not cover mixture, dilute 1 teaspoon salt in 1 cup water and add to cabbage).

Cover cabbage with a plate, then weigh down with a water-filled ziplock bag or other heavy weight, making sure all cabbage is submerged in liquid to prevent mold.

Cover the tub with a lid or a piece of cheesecloth or a dish towel secured with a rubber band and store in a cool, dark place for 1 week, checking daily to make sure liquid is still covering sauerkraut and that no mold has formed.

Transfer to an airtight container and refrigerate. Sauerkraut can be stored in refrigerator for up to 3 months.

Kraut Burgers

Makes 16 burgers

This German recipe is one my family has passed down from generation to generation. We like to take these along on picnics or short hikes for a quick meal on the go.

Dough

2 cups warm water

2¼ teaspoons (1 packet) active dry yeast

2 tablespoons evaporated cane juice crystals

1 teaspoon salt

2 tablespoons vegetable oil, plus more for rubbing on dough

4½ cups all-purpose flour, plus more if necessary

Filling

2 tablespoons olive oil

1 medium onion, chopped (1 cup)

1 pound cooked **Seitan Loaf** (recipe page 182), finely minced

3 cups **Sauerkraut** (recipe page 57), squeezed of excess liquid

2 tablespoons sesame or poppy seeds

Mustard or ketchup for serving

Make dough:

Place water, yeast, and cane juice crystals in a large bowl. Stir until dissolved, then let stand until foamy, 10 minutes.

Add salt and oil and stir. Add 2 cups of the flour and stir until incorporated. Add 2 more cups of flour and stir until spoon becomes difficult to work with, then mix with your hands. Continue adding flour a little at a time while kneading, until a soft, elastic dough is formed, 7 to 8 minutes. Form into a ball and rub with oil. Cover with a cloth and let rise until doubled in size (or even more), about 2 hours.

Make filling:

Heat oil in a medium skillet over medium-high heat. Sauté onion, stirring occasionally, until caramelized, 9 to 10 minutes. Add minced seitan and stir until browned and crisp, 4 to 5 minutes. Add sauerkraut and cook, stirring, until dry and combined, 2 to 3 minutes. Set aside.

Make burgers:

Preheat oven to 350°F.

Place dough on a lightly floured surface and roll to ⅓-inch thickness. Using a round cookie cutter or jar top, cut circles about 5 inches in diameter. Place ⅓ cup filling in the center of half of the circles, leaving a 1-inch border around the edge. Moisten edges with water, cover with another circle, and press edges lightly to seal. Place buns on a cookie sheet lined with parchment paper, leaving at least an inch between them. Cover with a clean towel and let sit for 20 minutes.

Spray tops with water and sprinkle with seeds. Bake until golden brown, turning the cookie sheet in the oven once after 15 minutes, 30 minutes total.

Serve with mustard or ketchup.

Raw Bok Choy and Black Radish Salad

Serves 6

At the Union Square Greenmarket in New York City and in Asian markets all over the place, there are sometimes as many as a dozen varieties of bok choy for sale. These days, it seems no one can get enough of its great flavor and crisp texture. Bok choy is great sautéed, but sometimes—especially in summer months—a no-cook salad does just the trick. This one is as much about color as it is about texture and flavor; the black-edged, mildly spicy radishes and creamy-green bok choy get a punch of additional color from a bit of red jalapeño.

¼ cup rice wine vinegar

2 tablespoons agave nectar

2 tablespoons toasted sesame oil

1 tablespoon soy sauce

1½ pounds Canton or Ching Chang bok choy, rinsed and chopped

1 black radish, skin-on, cut into matchsticks

½ small red jalapeño pepper, seeded and thinly sliced

2 tablespoons lightly toasted sesame seeds

1 tablespoon lightly toasted black sesame seeds

Whisk together vinegar, agave nectar, sesame oil, and soy sauce in a large bowl. Combine bok choy, radish, and jalapeño in a bowl and toss with dressing. Garnish with sesame seeds and black sesame seeds.

Za'atar-Roasted Kohlrabi

Serves 6

Ever since I saw kohlrabi for the first time as a kid—Dad grew both the green and purple varieties—I thought they looked like futuristic globes, their little antenna-like stems sticking out every which way. Though Mom served the crunchy, cabbage-like kohlrabi (the name is derived from the German words for "cabbage" and "turnip") for dinner once in a while, the raw bulbs were always a favorite field snack during harvesting. Here, the dusky combination of sumac, oregano, sesame seeds, and hyssop in the captivating za'atar spice blend cloaks the crunchy kohlrabi in a worthy coating.

4 kohlrabi bulbs, stems intact (about 2½ pounds)

3 tablespoons olive oil

2 tablespoons za'atar spice blend (available at Middle Eastern specialty stores and *www.penzeys.com*)

1 tablespoon lemon juice

½ teaspoon salt

½ teaspoon freshly ground black pepper

Preheat oven to 400°F.

Remove stems from kohlrabi and reserve for snacking (consider serving with Green Goddess Dressing, recipe page 40). Peel kohlrabi and cut each bulb into 12 wedges.

Whisk together olive oil, za'atar, lemon juice, salt, and pepper in a large bowl.

Add kohlrabi to the bowl and toss to coat. Transfer to a baking dish and roast, tossing every 15 minutes, until kohlrabi is tender and browned, 35 to 40 minutes.

Braised Cardoons and Red Endive

Serves 6

We're quite taken with cardoons, which often get mistaken for celery but have a mildly bitter flavor and history all their own. They have a two-thousand-year history as a weed that became a staple of *cucina povera* (peasant food) in Rome, and are very versatile if prepared properly. We sell two types: gorgeous, red-blushed Rouge d'Alger, and pale-white Gobbo di Nizzia. Just make sure to prepare them properly, by trimming off any thorns and leaves and peeling to remove the stringy outer fibers. Trust us: In this recipe, in which cardoons are braised with red endive, the results are worth the effort.

4 cups water	1½ cups vegetable broth
3 tablespoons lemon juice	1 tablespoon nutritional yeast
1 large bunch cardoons (5 cardoon stalks)	1 teaspoon chopped fresh marjoram
3 tablespoons olive oil, plus more for drizzling	1 teaspoon chopped fresh thyme
	½ teaspoon salt
6 red Belgian endive heads, trimmed	½ teaspoon freshly ground black pepper

Preheat oven to 425°F.

Combine water and lemon and bring to a boil. While water is boiling, remove leaves from cardoons, then remove stringy outer part of cardoon stalks with a peeler.

Cut cardoons into 4-inch lengths, then halve each length. Add cardoons to water and simmer until partially tender, 4 to 5 minutes. Drain and rinse under cold water.

Heat oil in a large saucepan over medium-high heat. Add cardoons and endive and cook, stirring as little as possible, until slightly golden, 3 to 4 minutes.

Add broth, yeast, marjoram, thyme, salt, and pepper. Cover, and bring to a boil.

Reduce heat to a simmer and cook until cardoons are tender and endive is wilted and soft, 20 to 25 minutes. Remove from heat and let sit for 10 minutes.

Drizzle with olive oil before serving.

Carrot Bread

Makes 2 loaves

When I was growing up on the farm, carrots were a late-winter treat. At a time when the ground was still mostly covered with snow, Dad would dig through the dirt and produce bright orange, green-topped roots out of the ground. We'd rub them off then roast them over an open fire. After a while they'd get really tender and caramelize a bit, and we could barely wait until they cooled off to taste them. They were as sweet as candy, and I don't think a carrot has tasted as good since. This carrot bread sure comes close.

3 cups unbleached all-purpose flour
1½ teaspoons baking soda
½ teaspoon baking powder
1 teaspoon salt
1¼ cups canola oil
¾ cup evaporated cane juice crystals
¾ cup brown sugar
1½ tablespoons Ener-G egg replacer, diluted in 6 tablespoons warm water

1 tablespoon vanilla
2 cups grated carrots
1 cup crushed pineapple with juice
1 cup lightly toasted chopped walnuts or pecans (optional)
Powdered sugar for dusting (optional)

Preheat oven to 325°F.

Grease and flour two 8- x 4-inch loaf pans and reserve. Whisk flour, baking soda, baking powder, and salt in a large bowl.

In a separate bowl whisk oil, crystals, brown sugar, reconstituted egg replacer, and vanilla until incorporated.

Stir in carrots, pineapple and juice, and walnuts until incorporated. Whisk together wet and dry ingredients until smooth and pour into prepared pans.

Bake until a toothpick inserted in the center comes out clean, 50 to 55 minutes. Let cool 5 minutes, transfer to baking racks, cool completely and dust with powdered sugar before serving.

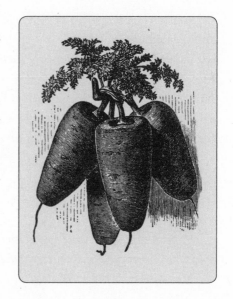

Fresh Pineapple and Carrot Salad with Candied Pecans

Makes 5 cups slaw

Draining the extra liquid out of the salad before adding the Vegenaise really makes a difference in the final product. For color variety, try Cosmic Purple, Snow White, or Atomic Red carrots mixed in with more common orange varieties. The candied pecans that go on top of the slaw are addictive—at Baker Creek about half of the sweet, toasty nuts disappear before they even make it into the bowl. Our advice: Make a double batch just in case.

Candied Pecans
½ cup roughly chopped pecans

2 tablespoons coconut oil

3 tablespoons evaporated cane juice crystals

¼ teaspoon cinnamon

Dash salt

Salad
4 cups shredded carrots (about 1¼ pounds)

2 cups finely diced fresh pineapple

1 medium apple, cored and finely diced

2 tablespoons fresh lime juice

1 teaspoon lime zest

¼ cup agave nectar

½ cup Vegenaise

⅛ teaspoon salt

Make candied pecans:
Stir pecans in a heavy skillet over medium heat until fragrant and lightly toasted, 4 to 5 minutes. Add coconut oil, crystals, cinnamon, and salt and cook, stirring, until sugar is melted and lightly browned, 2 to 3 minutes. Transfer to a lightly oiled cookie sheet and cool in a single layer, breaking candied nuts apart when completely cooled. Can be made up to 1 week ahead and stored in an airtight container.

Make salad:
Toss carrots, pineapple, apple, lime juice, lime zest, and agave nectar in a large bowl and let rest for 30 minutes.

Pour mixture into a colander and drain, pressing down with a wooden spoon remove as much liquid as possible. Return to bowl and add Vegenaise and salt.

Mix well and chill at least 30 minutes. Top with pecans before serving.

Maple Pie

Serves 8 to 10

Emilee and I often have friends over for weekend visits, and one way or the other we always seem to end up in the garden picking our supper together. This sweet treat is wonderful for fall and harvest festival celebrations—or all year round. This is the perfect ending to a delicious meal enjoyed by a houseful of loved ones. The carrot adds a lovely amber hue to the pie.

1 medium (4-ounce) carrot, grated (about ⅔ cup)

¼ cup water

¼ cup coconut oil

⅔ cup (6 ounces) pitted medjool dates

⅔ cup coconut milk

3 tablespoons maple syrup

2 teaspoons pure vanilla

½ teaspoon salt

1½ cups cold soymilk

4 tablespoons cornstarch

Prepared Graham Cracker Pie Crust (recipe page 66)

Combine carrots and water in a small saucepan. Bring to a boil, reduce heat, cover, and simmer until very soft, 10 minutes. Transfer to a blender. Add coconut oil and blend until smooth. Add dates, coconut milk, maple syrup, vanilla, and salt, and blend until smooth and thick, 30 seconds; reserve.

Whisk together soymilk and cornstarch in a medium saucepan and bring to a boil over medium heat. Reduce to a simmer and cook, stirring, until thickened, 1 minute. Add reserved blended mixture to thickened soymilk, return to a boil, reduce heat, and cook until thickened, an additional 1 to 2 minutes.

Pour into prepared Graham Cracker Pie Crust and chill, covered, 6 hours or up to 24 hours. Serve garnished with a few additional graham cracker crumbs and Coconut Whipped Cream (recipe page 176).

Graham Cracker Pie Crust

Makes 1 crust

Use this crust whenever you want to add a flavorful cookie base that can stand up to a creamy filling—think chocolate mousse, lemon, or the Maple Pie recipe that precedes this one.

12 Homemade Graham Crackers (recipe page 177)

⅓ cup melted coconut oil
¼ cup evaporated cane juice crystals

Preheat oven to 350°F.

Place graham crackers in a food processor and process until fine, 15 seconds (you should have about 1½ cups graham cracker crumbs).

Transfer to a bowl and toss to combine with coconut oil and cane juice crystals. Press into 9-inch pie dish and bake until golden brown, 8 to 9 minutes.

Remove from oven and cool completely.

Preserved Meyer Lemon–Cumin Moroccan Carrots

Serves 6

One of the reasons I love growing and harvesting carrots is because of how fresh, crisp, and juicy they are when they come out of the ground. It's true, they cellar well and can last you through the winter—but there is nothing like the fresh crunch of an hours-old carrot fresh from the ground. This is a love I've passed on to the next generation; Sasha, our daughter, is as much of a carrot fan as we are. When we make this refreshing salad, we always keep a few raw carrots around for snacking.

1¼ pounds (2 large) Atomic Red carrots, peeled and cut into ¼-inch coins

1¼ pounds (2 large) Amarillo carrots, peeled and cut into ¼-inch coins

3 tablespoons olive oil

2 Preserved Meyer Lemons (recipe page 68), chopped (about ⅓ cup)

3 tablespoons lemon juice, or more to taste

2 tablespoons finely chopped parsley

1 teaspoon ground cumin

1 clove finely minced garlic

½ teaspoon salt

¼ teaspoon freshly ground black pepper

Prepare a large ice water bath.

Bring a large pot of salted water to a boil. Add carrots and cook until just tender-crisp, 7 to 8 minutes. Drain and plunge carrots into ice water bath for 3 minutes to stop cooking and preserve color; drain and reserve.

Whisk together olive oil, Preserved Meyer Lemons, lemon juice, parsley, cumin, garlic, salt, and pepper. Toss reserved carrots with dressing and serve at room temperature.

Preserved Meyer Lemons

Makes 3 pints

Nothing could be easier or more versatile than these pucker-inducing lemons, which we love to add to soups, stews, and salads. They last for up to a year, and you'll be surprised at how often you turn to them to punch up all manner of dishes. You can use regular lemons if Meyers aren't available.

8 Meyer lemons	2 cups fresh lemon juice
1 cup kosher salt	3 tablespoons olive oil, divided

Scrub and dry lemons carefully. Cut each lemon in quarters, transfer to a bowl, and combine with salt.

Pack into three sterilized pint-sized jars and cover with lemon juice. Cover tightly with a sterilized jar top and let rest at room temperature (not a cold location) until lemons are cured, 1 week. Cover surface of each jar with 1 tablespoon oil to prevent mold, reseal, and refrigerate for up to 6 months.

Aloo Gobi with Potatoes and Cauliflower

Serves 6

After driving back and forth across the country several times the past few years, Emilee and I have learned that an Indian restaurant can be a downright oasis for traveling vegetarians and vegans. If you're hungry and driving and you don't know where to go, pull into the nearest Indian restaurant and choose from any number of vegetable dishes. Aloo Gobi, a cauliflower- and potato-studded main course, is a staple for our family. This recipe is filled with healthy nutrients, including fiber-rich potatoes and cauliflower and antioxidant-rich turmeric. It's also great for kids. Our daughter, Sasha, loves a little spice in her food, and this is one of her favorite meals. Our recipe is mildly spicy; if you prefer more heat, add more crushed red pepper to taste. Make sure to have all your spices and other ingredients carefully prepared in advance, since everything gets added in rapid succession.

1 medium cauliflower head (1½ pounds), cored, trimmed, and quartered

2½ pounds Yukon Gold potatoes

5 tablespoons safflower or vegetable oil

1 teaspoon whole brown mustard seeds

1 teaspoon whole yellow mustard seeds

¾ teaspoon whole cumin seeds

16 whole fenugreek seeds

1 dried red chili, crushed

1 large onion, finely diced (2 cups)

1 large Anaheim chili pepper, seeded and finely diced (about ½ cup)

1 teaspoon turmeric

1 teaspoon ground cumin

1 teaspoon ground coriander

2 teaspoons salt

1 tablespoon fresh crushed garlic

1 tablespoon minced fresh ginger

6 scallions, trimmed and cut into ½-inch pieces

2 tablespoons fresh cilantro leaves for garnish

Cooked basmati rice

Bring a large pot of water to a boil. Lower cauliflower pieces into water and blanch for 4 minutes. Remove with a large slotted spoon (do not discard boiling water) and cool completely; cut into smaller florets and reserve.

While cauliflower is cooling, cook potatoes in reserved boiling water just until tender, 25 to 30 minutes. Drain and cool 10 minutes, slip off skins and discard, and dice potatoes into 1-inch pieces. Combine with cauliflower in a large bowl.

In a large, heavy skillet, heat oil over medium heat, then add brown and yellow mustard seeds, cumin, and fenugreek and stir, being careful not to burn, until seeds begin to pop, 10 to 15 seconds. Add dried chili, then immediately add onions, Anaheim chili pepper, tumeric, cumin, coriander, and salt, and cook until the onion is translucent and peppers are softened, 7 to 8 minutes. Add garlic, ginger, and scallions and cook 1 additional minute. Remove from heat, drizzle over cooked potatoes and cauliflower, and gently stir until evenly coated; let stand for 10 minutes, or refrigerate up to 12 hours. Meanwhile, heat 2 large well-seasoned cast-iron skillets (or 1 oversized) over medium heat until hot. Divide mixture between the two skillets and cook until underside is lightly browned, 5 to 7 minutes, then flip and continue to cook until other side is browned, an additional 5 to 7 minutes.

Top with fresh cilantro if desired and serve immediately with rice and Creamy Armenian Cucumber Sauce (recipe page 74).

Herb-Roasted Cauliflower Steaks

Serves 4

I love the way this cauliflower gets almost meatlike when roasted until golden brown. These "steaks" are also wonderful at room temperature—try them in a sandwich with some zesty condiments. If you've got a garden full, use mineral-rich, buttery Purple of Sicily, or a more traditional white Giant of Naples—but plain old cauliflower from the farmers' market does the trick, too.

2 medium cauliflower heads (2½ to 3 pounds)

3 tablespoons olive oil

2 cloves minced garlic

2 tablespoons chopped fresh thyme

2 tablespoons chopped fresh oregano

1 tablespoon chopped fresh rosemary

1 tablespoon nutritional yeast

½ teaspoon chili flakes

1 teaspoon salt

½ teaspoon freshly ground black pepper

Preheat oven to 375°F. Using a sharp knife, carefully slice cauliflower into ½-inch-thick slices, including core. You will end up with 2 steaks from each cauliflower head, plus several cups of florets.

Combine olive oil, garlic, thyme, oregano, rosemary, yeast, chili flakes, salt, and pepper. Rub half of mixture on cauliflower steaks and toss florets with remaining mixture. Place in a single layer on baking sheets. Roast until golden brown and tender, turning once, 25 to 30 minutes total.

Serve with Tomato Gravy (recipe page 166).

Corn Dodgers with Edible Flowers

Makes 24

My grandmother Bertha was Mexican, and we ate a lot of corn tamales and tortillas—often homemade and always delicious. My dad grew 60 acres of corn every year on our property, and he dedicated a small part of the fields to a patch of rainbow corn, which blew my mind with its range of colors and tiny size. Hopi Blue corn, with colors that vary from medium to deep-purplish blue, was an early success, and as young as age 12, I was shucking, husking, and grinding meal from dried kernels, and even making cornbread. These corn dodgers are a family favorite, and are perfect for your breakfast or brunch rotation. The Indonesian Kennikura Cosmos flower adds a touch of color to this delicious dish. Part hush puppy and part fritter, the dodgers positively burst with the goodness of fresh corn, no matter what variety you choose to use. Just make sure you use organic, non-GMO corn for this recipe, as most commercial corn is contaminated with genetically modified toxins.

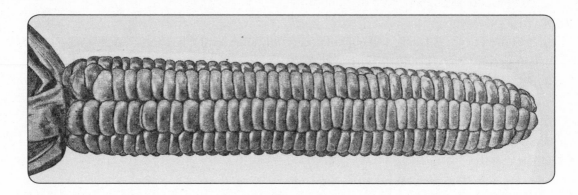

4 scallions, trimmed, whites and greens separated

5 tablespoons coconut oil, divided

2 cloves minced garlic

2 cups unbleached all-purpose flour

1 tablespoon baking powder

½ teaspoon salt

1 cup coconut milk

1 tablespoon maple syrup

1 cup fresh corn kernels (from 2 ears corn)

1 ounce edible Indonesian Kennikura Cosmos flowers, petals plucked

¼ cup water

Vegetable oil for frying

Slice scallion whites and greens separately and reserve in separate bowls. Heat 2 tablespoons coconut oil in a heavy skillet over medium heat. Cook scallion whites, stirring often, until lightly browned, 5 to 6 minutes. Add garlic and cook an additional minute. Remove from heat and reserve.

Combine flour, baking powder, and salt in a large bowl. In a separate bowl whisk together coconut milk, remaining 3 tablespoons coconut oil, maple syrup, corn kernels, flower petals, and reserved scallion greens. Combine wet and dry ingredients, then gradually add water 1 tablespoon at a time until a thick pancake batter forms.

Heat ¼ inch oil in a cast-iron skillet over medium-high heat. Drop batter 2 tablespoons at a time into the hot oil and fry until lightly browned and crisp, 2 to 3 minutes per side. Repeat with remaining batter, adding more oil as necessary. Drain on paper towels and cover with foil to keep warm.

Creamy Armenian Cucumber Sauce

Makes 2 cups

This is our version of the traditional Indian condiment raita. My sister, Jessica, created this recipe to tame down our favorite spicy foods so that guests less enthusiastic about fiery dishes could comfortably enjoy an authentic Indian meal without sounding three alarms.

1 teaspoon whole cumin seeds

1 cup Soy Sour Cream (recipe page 180)

⅔ cup seeded, diced Armenian cucumber

2 tablespoons freshly squeezed lemon juice, plus more if desired

1 teaspoon minced garlic

2 teaspoons minced chives, plus more for garnish

Place cumin seeds in a dry skillet over medium-low heat and cook, shaking occasionally, until seeds begin to pop and are lightly browned, 1 to 2 minutes.

Remove from heat and cool. In a medium-sized bowl, combine Soy Sour Cream, cucumber, lemon juice, garlic, chives, and cumin seeds and stir until incorporated.

Chill for at least 1 hour. Thin with additional lemon juice or water to taste. Transfer to a bowl and garnish with additional chives.

Cambodian Yellow Cucumber Salad with Crispy Shallots

Serves 4

One of the first crops I ever grew was cucumbers. Poring over seed catalogs as a kid, I discovered that they were easy to grow, and I was hooked. I tried Lemon cucumbers, which looked just like citrus but were sweet and mild; White Wonders, originally introduced by W. Atlee Burpee in 1893; and lots of others. Now I plant 6 or 7 varieties every year, always looking for something new and interesting to bring to our customers and into my own kitchen. This spicy salad, inspired by ones you'll find all over Cambodia, works especially well with some of the Southeast Asian cucumber varieties, such as Hmong Red, Sikkim, and Chinese Yellow. They're crunchy, fresh-tasting, and can hold their own both in salads and for pickling.

2 tablespoons vegetable oil

2 shallots, very thinly sliced (about ½ cup)

2 yellow cucumbers (see varieties above), about 1 pound, scrubbed, peels on

1 tablespoon salt

2 scallions, greens and whites, very thinly sliced

⅓ cup rice vinegar

⅓ cup evaporated cane juice crystals

¼ cup whole cilantro leaves

1 hot pepper, seeded and very thinly sliced

3 tablespoons chopped peanuts

Heat oil in a saucepan over medium-high heat. Fry shallots until crisp, 7 minutes. Drain on paper towels and reserve. Thinly slice cucumbers and place in a bowl with salt. Let sit for 30 minutes, rinse lightly, drain, and squeeze out excess moisture. Combine in a bowl with scallions, vinegar, cane juice crystals, cilantro, and pepper. Top with peanuts and reserved crispy shallots.

Baba Ghanoush

Makes 2½ cups

In Middle Eastern and Mediterranean countries, there are more ways to make eggplant than you can shake a stick at. One of the best is baba ghanoush, pureed eggplant seasoned with a variety of spices and other additives to make a creamy, addictive spread. I like mine smoky, so I either toast the eggplants until the skins char, or, when I'm feeling brave (and not afraid of cleanup), I char them on my stovetop, turning them until black. After scooping out the creamy pulp, in goes tahini, lemon, garlic—there couldn't be a more perfect combination. Many heirloom eggplants are perfect for this recipe; feel free to use Black Beauty, Rosa Bianca, Apple Green, or Rosita varieties.

2 large Black Beauty or Rosa Bianca eggplants, or other varieties, see above (about 2½ pounds)

3 tablespoons Homemade Tahini (recipe page 178), plus more to taste

2 tablespoons fresh lemon juice, plus more to taste

1 teaspoon finely minced garlic

1 teaspoon salt

½ teaspoon freshly ground black pepper

Pita bread and falafel fixings

Prick eggplant all over with a fork.

Turn on the stovetop burner to medium heat and place eggplant over burner grate, turning occasionally until skin is charred and flaky, 15 to 20 minutes (alternately, preheat oven to broil, place eggplant on a foil-lined baking sheet and bake, turning, until eggplant skin is blackened and eggplant is puffy and soft when pierced with a skewer, 25 to 30 minutes).

Transfer eggplant to a bowl, cover, and cool for 30 minutes.

Drain liquid from bowl, then peel skin and discard skin and seeds from eggplant.

Roughly chop eggplant (or puree in a food processor for smoother results) and return to bowl. Add Homemade Tahini, lemon juice, garlic, salt, and pepper, then season to taste. Serve with fresh pita bread or falafel sandwiches.

Breaded Heirloom Eggplant Cutlets

Serves 6

Emilee says:

When I was dating Jere, I was relatively new to vegan cooking, and working to adjust my lifestyle and favorite recipes to a new way of life. I remember visiting Jere's sister, Jessica, and watching as she cooked up these eggplant cutlets. My run-ins with eggplant up to that point hadn't been very positive, so I was a bit skeptical. But when I tasted this family favorite, I was delighted and asked for seconds. The mild, buttery flavor of the eggplant accentuated by a crunchy topping is so satisfying. Even the most staunch eggplant critic will love this tried-and-tested recipe. We love to serve these topped with our delicious Heirloom Shallot Tomato Sauce alongside hot angel hair pasta, a fresh garden salad, and crusty garlic bread.

1 large Aswad or Ping Tung eggplant,
    (1¼ to 1½ pounds), cut into 12 half-inch
    slices

½ teaspoon salt
½ teaspoon garlic powder
¼ teaspoon freshly ground black pepper
¼ cup olive oil, divided

Breading
5 thick slices vegan country white bread,
    torn into pieces, or 2½ cups vegan
    panko bread crumbs
⅓ cup nutritional yeast flakes

Batter
1 cup Vegenaise
¼ cup large-grained Dijon mustard
½ teaspoon freshly ground black pepper

Preheat oven to 350°F.

Make breading:
Place bread in a food processor and pulse until crumbs form, 25 to 30 seconds. Transfer crumbs or panko to a bowl and combine with nutritional yeast, salt, garlic powder, and pepper.

Make batter:
Combine Vegenaise, mustard, and pepper in a bowl and whisk until smooth.

Make cutlets:

Brush a 10- x 15-inch cookie sheet with 2 tablespoons of the olive oil.

Place eggplant slices in batter and turn to coat both sides. Transfer to breading mix, scooping crumbs over and around eggplant to cover completely; press lightly to coat sides and edges well.

Place breaded eggplant slices 1 inch apart on cookie sheet, brush with remaining oil, and bake until browned and crisp on one side, 20 to 25 minutes.

With a flat spatula, carefully flip slices and bake until the other side is crisp, an additional 20 minutes.

Ping Tung Eggplant Cake

Serves 12

Long, slender, lavender-colored Ping Tung eggplant is our favorite variety here at Baker Creek, and it finds its way into the kitchen almost every day when it's in season. I love its glossy lavender skin, mild flavor, and creamy flesh—as well as its versatility. One year we were blessed with such an abundant harvest that we had to figure out what to do with the excess. Our restaurant chef came up with a rather ingenious way of using it up: in a dessert. When we ask our guests to guess the mystery ingredient, they're almost always shocked to discover that it's pureed eggplant. This rich, dense confection has become a favorite dessert at the restaurant, and we like to think of ourselves as ambassadors for one of our favorite vegetables.

1 cup canola oil, divided

4 large or 6 medium Ping Tung egg-plants, peeled and chopped (about 6 cups)

3 cups unbleached all-purpose flour

1½ cups evaporated cane juice crystals

½ cup brown sugar

1 teaspoon baking powder

1 teaspoon baking soda

1 teaspoon salt

1½ tablespoons Ener-G egg replacer, dissolved in 6 tablespoons cold water

2 teaspoons vanilla extract

Preheat oven to 350°F.

In a large skillet, heat 2 tablespoons oil over medium-high heat and cook eggplant, stirring occasionally, until tender, 7 to 8 minutes. Remove from heat, cool slightly, and puree in a food processor until smooth, 10 to 15 seconds; you should have about 2 cups eggplant puree.

In a medium-sized bowl, whisk together flour, cane juice crystals, brown sugar, baking powder, baking soda, and salt. In a separate bowl, combine eggplant puree, remaining oil, reconstituted egg replacer, and vanilla. Add to dry mixture and stir until well blended. Pour into a well-oiled Bundt pan and bake until a toothpick inserted into the center comes out clean, 50 to 55 minutes. Cool for 10 minutes, then invert to a wire rack and cool completely.

Heirloom Roasted Eggplant Pizza

Makes 2 pizzas

Spreading hummus on top of pizza instead of tomato sauce may sound strange—but don't knock it until you try it. When baked, the hummus adapts a texture and flavor that's simultaneously nutty, toasty, and creamy. Adding olives, tomatoes, and eggplant rounds out the Mediterranean character of these pies—a real departure from standard pizzeria fare.

Pizza Crust
1½ cups water, divided
1¼ teaspoons active dry yeast
1 teaspoon agave nectar
4 cups unbleached all-purpose flour, divided, plus more for kneading
2 teaspoons salt

Eggplant
¼ cup olive oil
2 cloves minced garlic

¼ teaspoon salt
¼ teaspoon freshly ground black pepper
3 Sicilian or small globe eggplants (about 1¼ pounds), sliced into ¼-inch-thick slices

Pizzas
2 tablespoons olive oil
1 cup hummus
½ cup sundried tomatoes
½ cup olives

Make pizza crust:
In a large bowl combine ½ cup water, yeast, and agave nectar.

Add ½ cup flour, stir, and let sit, covered with plastic wrap, until slightly foamy, 10 minutes.

Whisk 3 additional cups flour with salt in a separate bowl. Gradually incorporate into yeast mixture, alternating with up to 1 cup additional water until a sticky ball of dough has formed.

Turn dough out onto a floured board and knead, working the remaining ½ cup of flour into the dough and kneading until smooth, pliable, and no longer sticky, 10 to 12 minutes.

Place dough in a large bowl and cover with plastic wrap. Let rise in a warm place until doubled, about 2 hours.

Make eggplant:
Preheat oven to 450°F.

Combine olive oil, garlic, salt, and pepper in a bowl. Brush both sides of eggplant with oil mixture and place on baking sheet.

Place eggplant in oven and bake until slightly softened, 5 to 6 minutes. Raise oven temperature to 525°F. Roast until eggplant begins to brown, an additional 3 to 4 minutes. Flip and roast until top side is browned, another 3 to 4 minutes. Remove from oven, transfer to a plate, and reserve. Place a pizza stone in oven to preheat.

Finish pizzas:

Remove dough from the bowl, punch down, and divide into 4 pieces. Wrap 2 pieces tightly in plastic wrap and freeze for a later use.

Place 1 piece of dough on a lightly floured surface. With a floured rolling pin, roll dough until 14 inches in diameter. Place on a pizza screen and let rest for 15 minutes; repeat with remaining dough ball.

Brush each pizza crust with 1 tablespoon olive oil, then top each one with ½ cup hummus. Sprinkle each pizza with ¼ cup sundried tomatoes and olives, then arrange half the eggplant on each pizza. Turn oven down to 450°F and bake pizza on a pizza stone until the crust has lightly browned, 18 to 20 minutes. Remove from oven and let stand 8 minutes before cutting. Serve immediately.

Fennel, Apple, and Cucumber Salad

Serves 6

Biting into a Pink Pearl apple is a wonderful surprise. Its flesh is a deep blushing pink that's as pleasing to the eye as it is to the palate, and it's got interesting flavor notes of cranberry and wine best showcased raw. This salad contrasts the color and crunchy tart-sweetness of the apples with licorice-scented fennel and cooling ribbons of cucumber. Using a mandoline slicer or Japanese benriner makes shaving the fennel and cucumber a snap. If you can't find Pink Pearls, try crisp, tart Fujis or Granny Smiths.

¼ cup fresh lime juice

¼ cup extra virgin olive oil

½ teaspoon kosher salt

¼ teaspoon freshly ground black pepper

2 fennel bulbs (about 1 pound), trimmed, some fronds reserved

½ English cucumber (about ½ pound), scrubbed

2 medium Pink Pearl apples, peeled and cored

1 tablespoon chopped fresh dill

Whisk together lime juice, olive oil, salt, and pepper in a bowl and reserve. Using a mandoline, thinly shave fennel into a bowl. Using the same slicer, slice cucumber lengthwise into ribbons. Cut the apples into matchsticks and add to fennel and cucumber. Add dressing and dill and toss gently. Serve scattered with fennel fronds.

Grilled Fennel with Tropical Tamarind Sauce

Serves 6 as an appetizer

In California, one of my favorite activities is hiking along the rugged Sonoma County coastline, harvesting wild fennel as I go and eating it as a snack. There's something about the contrast of the pale-green bulbs against the delicate, dill-like fronds that mesmerizes me every time, and I love the subtle anise flavor and snappy crunch. I can't always get out to the coast to pick it myself, so we keep fennel growing in our personal garden as much as possible. Grilling it brings out its licorice-like characteristics and changes the texture in surprising ways.

Tropical Tamarind Sauce
⅔ cup tamarind concentrate
⅔ cup pineapple juice
2 teaspoons minced garlic
2 teaspoons minced ginger
¼ teaspoon ground allspice or cardamom
⅛ teaspoon salt

Fennel
2 heads fennel (about 1½ pounds), stalks trimmed, some fronds reserved
1 tablespoon vegetable oil
½ teaspoon salt
¼ teaspoon freshly ground black pepper

Make Tropical Tamarind Sauce:
Combine all ingredients in a small saucepan. Bring to a boil, reduce heat, and simmer, stirring to avoid burning, until slightly thickened, 3 to 4 minutes.

Prepare fennel:
Heat a grill or grill pan over medium-high heat. Cut fennel into ¼-inch slices. Brush with oil and sprinkle with salt and pepper. Grill until tender-crisp and grill marks have formed, 5 to 6 minutes per side. Divide among 6 plates and serve with Tropical Tamarind Sauce.

Caramelized Figs with Maple Cream and Crystallized Ginger

Serves 4

This dessert is simplicity personified, and one you'll turn to again and again in fig season. The maple cream is a snap to whip up—make extra to have on hand whenever you need to add a sweet touch—and broiling the figs makes such a difference in enhancing their flavor. Black Mission, Brown Turkey, or Violette de Bordeaux varieties all do the trick, but we like green figs such as Diana, Flanders, or Peter's Honey, too. Trees of Antiquity, a seller of heirloom fruit trees (*www.treesofantiquity.com*) has a wonderful selection of trees you can plant yourself.

1 cup Soy Sour Cream (recipe page 180)

2 tablespoons maple syrup

12 large, ripe figs

½ cup brown sugar or turbinado sugar

2 tablespoons chopped Crystallized Ginger (recipe page 85)

Preheat oven to broil. Combine Soy Sour Cream and maple syrup in a small bowl and chill.

Place figs on a foil-lined baking sheet (make sure it fits in your broiler). Cut a large "✕" in the top of each fig and sprinkle evenly with sugar.

Broil until sugar bubbles slightly and figs split open, 2 to 4 minutes, depending on your broiler.

Remove from oven and cool slightly.

Place 3 figs on each of 4 dessert plates and top with a dollop of maple cream. Sprinkle with crystallized ginger.

Crystallized Ginger or Galangal

Makes 3½ cups

Who knew something so good was so easy? I'd seen candied citrus peel recipes over the years but never realized you could use a similar procedure to make candy out of humble ginger root. It's a great digestive after a meal and can also be packaged in cellophane bags, tied with a ribbon, and given as gifts for the holidays or anytime. Some people boil the ginger a few times to remove its heat, but it's precisely that spicy kick that I relish so much. This recipe would also work well with galangal, the mellower, more floral version of ginger that you find all over Southeast Asia, and which is sometimes available at farmers' markets.

4 cups water
4½ cups evaporated cane juice crystals, divided

1 large piece ginger (about 1 pound) or galangal, peeled and very thinly sliced

Combine water and 4 cups cane juice crystals in a medium saucepan, bring to a boil, and reduce heat to a simmer. Add ginger and cook until ginger has absorbed much of the syrup, 45 to 50 minutes.

Remove from heat, strain ginger from liquid, and dry ginger on wire racks for 30 minutes. Place remaining crystals in a ziplock bag, then shake ginger in bag until well coated with crystals. Return to wire rack until completely dried, an additional 2 to 4 hours. Store in an airtight container for up to 3 months.

Garlic Naan Bread

Makes 6 naan breads

Naan bread is always one of my favorite parts of an Indian meal, and this recipe has been perfected over time. We add lots of garlic and scallions for color and flavor. Many people think there's just one kind of garlic, but we know different. Sarah Shimizu, an heirloom garlic grower in Orleans, California, agrees. She recommends either Purple Glazer or Inchelium Red varieties—both of which take well to roasting and baking, losing any sharp aftertaste and leaving behind a garlicky sweetness that melds perfectly into this soft, tender dough.

1 teaspoon Sucanat crystals	¼ teaspoon salt
1 teaspoon active dry yeast	4 tablespoons coconut oil, divided
¾ cup warm water	3 tablespoons coconut milk
1½ cups all-purpose flour, plus more for kneading	4 garlic cloves, thinly sliced
	2 scallions, thinly sliced

Combine Sucanat and yeast in a small bowl and add water. Stir to dissolve yeast and let sit until mixture is foamy, 10 minutes.

In a separate bowl combine flour and salt. Stir in 2 tablespoons of the coconut oil and the coconut milk, then pour in the yeast mixture and knead with your hands to form a dough ball.

Turn out onto a lightly floured surface and knead until smooth and no longer sticky, 5 minutes.

Return dough to a lightly oiled bowl, cover, and let rest until doubled, 1½ to 2 hours.

Preheat oven to 550°F. Line a baking sheet with aluminum foil and brush with some of the remaining coconut oil.

Turn dough onto a floured surface, punch, add garlic and scallions, and knead for 2 minutes, working in scallions.

Break off small portions of the dough and use a rolling pin to roll into six 6-inch-wide, ½-inch-thick discs.

Place dough onto greased foil, brush with coconut oil and bake, turning once when underside is cooked and edges are very lightly browned, after 3 to 4 minutes. Brush again with remaining coconut oil and return to oven until cooked through but not too brown, an additional 3 to 4 minutes.

Serve warm, sprinkled with additional salt if desired.

Amaranth Breakfast Pudding

Makes about 5 cups

Amaranth grain may be super nutritious—it's high in iron, the antioxidant lysine, and high-quality protein—but its appeal goes far beyond that. It has a crunchy pop even when cooked, and it takes on flavor with ease. We flavor this amaranth breakfast cereal (if you're harvesting your own seed, plant a variety such as our Hartman's Giant) with almond milk and agave nectar, but it's so versatile you could swap the liquid for coconut milk, soymilk, or rice milk and use the sweetener of your choice. If you don't finish all of the cereal, you can reheat it and thin it out by adding more almond milk.

1 cup amaranth grain	¼ teaspoon salt
3 cups water	1 cup fresh blueberries
2 cups plain almond milk	½ cup toasted slivered almonds
¼ cup dark agave nectar	

Bring amaranth and water to a boil, reduce heat and simmer until most liquid is absorbed and amaranth is plump but not totally cooked, about 20 minutes. Add almond milk, agave nectar, and salt, stir to incorporate, and cook until mixture forms large bubbles, an additional 5 minutes. Divide among bowls and serve warm, topped with blueberries and almonds.

Spelt Crackers

Makes 1 large cracker sheet

Inspired by a recipe that we saw in the *New York Times* a few years ago, these crackers have become a favorite. You just knead, roll, top (our choice additions are sunflower seeds, flaxseed, and flaky Maldon sea salt, which add just the right amount of crunch to the already nutty spelt flour), and bake. The original recipe called for scoring the dough, but we like just breaking off pieces of the baked crackers and snacking on them throughout the day.

1¼ cups spelt flour, plus extra
    for flouring surface
¾ teaspoon salt
½ cup cold water

1 teaspoon Maldon sea salt or
    other flaky sea salt
¼ cup sunflower seeds
2 teaspoons flaxseeds

Preheat oven to 350°F.

Whisk together flour and salt. Add water and stir until a stiff ball of dough forms, adding more flour if necessary.

Lightly flour a 10- x 17-inch flat cookie sheet and roll the dough directly on the sheet, sprinkling flour on top of dough as necessary, until dough is evenly rolled and as thin as possible.

Using a spray bottle, mist dough with water, then sprinkle with Maldon sea salt, sunflower seeds, and flaxseeds.

Bake until dough is crisp and lightly browned and cracker sheet can be lifted in one piece from cookie sheet, 20 to 25 minutes.

Cool completely and snap into pieces.

Farro-Endive-Pear Salad with Pecans and Lemony Thyme Vinaigrette

Serves 8

Imported from Italy, farro—also known as emmer wheat—lasts well in the pantry, owing to its lack of natural oils and hearty growing conditions. It's an ancient grain that has been unearthed at archaeological digs around the world, including Turkey, Israel, and Greece. Here, we pair it with crunchy endive and red onion, sweet pear, and crunchy nuts, for a salad that's great year-round but especially satisfying come autumn.

1½ cups farro

5 tablespoons fresh lemon juice

2 teaspoons Dijon mustard

1 teaspoon agave nectar

¾ teaspoon salt

½ teaspoon freshly ground black pepper

½ cup olive oil

4 endive heads, outer leaves removed and discarded

1 red-skinned pear, cored and diced (about 1 cup)

½ small red onion, very thinly sliced

1 tablespoon finely chopped crystallized ginger

1 tablespoon chopped fresh thyme

⅔ cup lightly toasted pecans

Bring a large pot of salted water to a boil. Add farro and cook until tender but not mushy, 25 to 30 minutes. Drain into a colander and cool.

While farro is cooking, whisk together lemon juice, mustard, agave nectar, salt, and pepper in a medium-sized bowl. Whisk in the olive oil in a slow stream until dressing is creamy; reserve.

Trim endive and slice into ¼-inch ribbons. Add to warm farro along with pear, onion, ginger, and thyme. Toss with dressing.

Top with pecans and season with additional salt and pepper just before serving.

Quinoa- and Tofu-Stuffed Cabbage Rolls

Makes 8 rolls

Peruvian Indians have been growing quinoa for thousands of years in the Andes Mountains. For vegans like us, quinoa is a miracle food. It's got as many essential amino acids as does meat, and it's super-versatile in salads, soups—and here, in a traditional sweet-and-sour stuffed cabbage recipe. The diced tofu and quinoa absorb the delicious tangy sauce, and there's extra liquid on the bottom to spoon over any leftover quinoa you may have cooked to make the recipe. Traditional Brunswick cabbage from our catalog works great, and try the trick of pre-freezing the cabbage head, which makes the leaves pliable, rollable, and super-easy to work with.

1 small head green cabbage (about 1½ pounds)	¾ teaspoon salt, divided
1 14.5-ounce block extra-firm tofu	1 teaspoon freshly ground black pepper, divided
1 medium carrot, finely shredded (about 1½ cups)	3 tablespoons canola oil
1 very large onion, finely chopped (about 3 cups), divided	4 cups tomato sauce
	½ cup fresh lemon juice
4 cloves minced garlic, divided	1 cup Sucanat crystals
2 cups cooked red quinoa	½ cup raisins
	¼ cup water

Place whole cabbage head in a ziplock bag and place in freezer for 4 hours or up to 2 days.

Wrap tofu block in a double layer of paper towels and place between two flat plates. Weigh down with a heavy object. Drain every few minutes until tofu has lost much of its additional moisture, 30 minutes to 1 hour. Finely mince and reserve.

Bring a large pot of water to a boil. Remove cabbage from freezer and place whole cabbage head in pot—whole leaves will come off easily. Working from root, remove 8 large outer leaves one at a time, being careful not to tear. Pat dry and reserve. Defrost remainder of cabbage in hot water for 5 minutes. Remove, drain, shred, and reserve.

Combine tofu, carrot, 1 cup onions, 2 cloves minced garlic, quinoa, and ½ teaspoon each salt and pepper in a bowl and mix with hands to incorporate. Place about ½ cup mixture in the center of each cabbage leaf. Pull bottom over filling, fold over side, then roll tightly (like a burrito). Repeat with other cabbage rolls and reserve.

To make the sauce, heat oil in a large (at least 6-quart) saucepan over medium heat. Add remaining 2 cups onions and cook, stirring, until soft, about 8 minutes. Add remaining garlic and cook an additional minute. Add shredded cabbage and cook, stirring, 2 more minutes. Add tomato sauce, lemon juice, Sucanat, raisins, water, and remaining salt and pepper. Bring to a boil, reduce heat, and simmer for 10 minutes until sauce thickens slightly. Gently lower cabbage rolls into sauce, pressing down so sauce covers rolls and spooning additional sauce over rolls if necessary. Cover tightly, reduce flame to very low, and simmer until rolls have absorbed much of the sauce, about 1½ hours. Remove from heat and serve with additional sauce.

Granny's Wild Possum Grape Jelly

Makes 4 pints

My mom makes this jelly out of the wild grapes that grow throughout the Ozark hills that surround our farm. She sells her jarred concoction in the bakery at Baker Creek, much to the delight of her customers. If wild grapes don't grow around your neck of the woods, try using a good-quality grape juice plus ¼ cup lemon juice as a substitute for the tangy wild grape juice.

4 cups wild grape juice, or good-quality unsweetened grape juice plus ¼ cup fresh lemon juice

7 cups evaporated cane juice crystals
1 3-ounce pouch liquid pectin

Stir together juice and cane juice crystals in a large saucepan.

Bring to a full boil, add pectin, and bring to a hard boil for 1 minute.

To test doneness, transfer a spoonful of jelly to the back of a plate. If it dries and stays in place, your jelly is done. If it runs down the plate, jelly needs more cooking time.

Pour into hot, prepared pint jars. Skim any foam from the top and adjust lids. Process for ten minutes in a water bath canner, remove, and cool completely before labeling.

Sometimes, no matter how carefully you follow instructions, jellies don't set as they're supposed to. Don't fret; by following a few simple instructions, you can fix your jelly. This is a technique we learned, as we did many others, from the *Ball Canning Guide*:

- For each cup of jelly that needs to be reprocessed, measure out 3 tablespoons sugar, ½ tablespoon lemon juice, and ½ tablespoon liquid pectin.
- Heat jelly in a saucepan over medium heat, just to a boil (stir often). Add sugar, lemon juice, and pectin and whisk until dissolved.
- Bring back to a hard boil and boil 1 minute, skimming foam if needed.
- Reprocess in sterilized jars as specified.

Concord Grape Simple Syrup

Makes 1½ cups

Come fall, one of my favorite fruits is the humble Concord grape. It's got a flavor all its own, so "grapey" that people sometimes think it's artificially derived. When I find them at the farmers' market, I inevitably overbuy—giving me the opportunity to make this syrup. Stir it into a glass of seltzer with a splash of lime juice, and you've got the best grape soda you've ever tasted.

   ¾ pound (2 cups) Concord grapes, washed
   ½ cup water
   1 cup evaporated cane juice crystals

Combine grapes, water, and cane juice crystals in a saucepan.

   Bring to a boil, reduce heat, and simmer, crushing grapes with the back of a spoon, until mixture thickens, 6 to 7 minutes.

   Remove from heat, strain syrup from solids through a fine-mesh strainer, discard solids, and cool syrup.

   Syrup can be stored, refrigerated, in an airtight container for up to 1 month.

Creamed Spinach and Lamb's Quarters

Makes 5 cups

At first glance lamb's quarters (supposedly named for their resemblance to a butcher's cut of mutton) may seem like nothing more than weeds, but once you taste them, you'll be as hooked as we are. They've got an earthy, mineral-rich flavor and cook up nice and easy like spinach. This recipe proves that creamed spinach isn't just a steakhouse staple—we love it here at Baker Creek, too. Most recipes call for lots of heavy cream or milk, which we replace with silken tofu, soymilk, and olive oil. The result is silky and delicious—a great side dish, or even a main course if you top it with toasted bread crumbs.

1 pound fresh baby spinach leaves

1 pound fresh lamb's quarters leaves

1 12-ounce package soft silken tofu

2 cups unsweetened soymilk

¼ cup nutritional yeast

1 teaspoon salt

½ teaspoon freshly ground black pepper

¼ teaspoon nutmeg

½ cup olive oil

4 cloves garlic, thinly sliced

Bring a large pot of water to a rolling boil. Add spinach and lamb's quarters leaves in batches, pushing down to submerge in water, until just wilted, 2 to 3 minutes. Transfer to a colander and drain. When cool enough to handle, squeeze out all excess moisture with your hands.

While leaves are cooling, place tofu, soymilk, nutritional yeast, salt, pepper, and nutmeg in a blender and puree until smooth, 10 seconds; reserve. Heat oil in a large sauté pan over medium heat. Add garlic and cook, stirring, until golden, 1 to 2 minutes. Add tofu mixture, stir, and warm over low heat until bubbling, 2 minutes. Add spinach and lamb's quarters leaves, stir, and simmer until leaves have absorbed some of the liquid, 3 to 4 minutes.

Rainbow Chard, Grape, and Delicata Squash Salad with Pumpkin Oil-Lime Dressing

Serves 4 as a generous appetizer

For a fancy dinner party, this composed salad gets raves, but how could it be any other way? Tender, green-striped Delicata squash, which make as pretty a centerpiece as a meal, is easy to find these days at farmers' markets. The squash gets roasted (and eaten) skin-on. Instead of wilting or cooking it, rainbow chard—white, yellow, and red stalks included—is left raw for maximum flinty effect, and toasted pepitas and juicy red grapes add a lingering sweetness and crunch. The real x-factor ingredient here is pumpkin seed oil; it's like a cross between the squash and the pumpkin seeds in one luscious package, and it ties the whole dish together.

Dressing
5 tablespoons pumpkin seed oil
2 tablespoons lime juice
¼ teaspoon salt
¼ teaspoon freshly ground black pepper
½ teaspoon agave nectar

Salad
2 small (1 pound each) Honeyboat
   Delicata squash, skin-on, halved,
   seeded, and cut into 6 wedges

2 tablespoons olive oil
1 teaspoon salt
½ teaspoon freshly ground black pepper
1 bunch rainbow chard (about ¾ pound),
   rinsed and dried
2 cups cooked quinoa
½ cup red seedless grapes, halved if
   small, quartered if large
¼ cup lightly toasted pepitas

Make dressing:
Whisk together pumpkin oil, lime juice, salt, pepper, and agave nectar until creamy and emulsified; reserve.

Make salad:
Preheat oven to 425°F. Toss squash with olive oil, salt, and pepper. Place on a baking sheet and

roast, turning once, until tender and golden on edges, 30 to 35 minutes. Remove from oven and cool to room temperature.

Cut chard leaves in half lengthwise (do not remove stems). Thinly shred leaves horizontally; you should end up with about 4 to 4½ cups chard. Combine with quinoa and 2 tablespoons prepared dressing.

Arrange about 1 cup chard-quinoa mixture on each of 4 plates. Top each plate with 3 squash wedges, 2 tablespoons grapes, and 1 tablespoon pepitas. Drizzle each salad with about 1 tablespoon remaining dressing.

Sautéed Rainbow Chard with Lemon and Pine Nuts

Serves 4

We love chard so much that we grow it in our greenhouse throughout the winter; its splashy colors and versatility have won us over. Truly a beautiful vegetable, chard provides hours of entertainment for Sasha as she sorts through the pink, orange, white, and red stalks, creating bunches that look as much like bouquets of flowers as healthy, leafy greens.

1 large or 2 small bunch rainbow chard (about between ¾ pound and 1 pound total), leaves separated from stalks
1 tablespoon extra virgin olive oil
1 tablespoon thinly sliced garlic

½ teaspoon salt
¼ teaspoon chili flakes
¼ teaspoon freshly ground black pepper
¼ cup toasted pine nuts
Lemon wedges for serving

Chop chard stalks and reserve. Roll leaves into a log and slice into ½-inch thin ribbons.

Heat oil in a large (12- or 14-inch) nonstick skillet over medium-high heat (a regular skillet works fine, too).

Add garlic and cook until fragrant and color just turns light brown, 15 to 30 seconds.

Add the chard stems and cook, stirring until stems are tender-crisp, 3 to 4 minutes.

Add the leaves and cook, stirring, until just wilted, 1 minute (add in 2 batches if necessary). Add salt, chili flakes, and pepper and cook an additional minute.

Transfer to a plate and garnish with toasted pine nuts.

Serve with lemon wedges.

Smoky Sautéed Collard Greens

Serves 4

I guess you could say that we are collard green elitists. Having grown them for so long, we relish their earthy flavor and nutritional benefits. On Baker Creek we grow the Georgia Southern Creole variety, an heirloom that's been around since before the 1880s and has a great, plucked-from-the-earth mineral flavor profile. Lately we've been smitten with Morris Heading collards, a waxy, looser-leafed variety that only grows sweeter the more frost it takes on.

4 bunches Morris Heading, Georgia Southern Creole, or other collard greens (about 4 pounds), stems removed and discarded

⅓ cup olive oil

2 torpedo shallots, thinly sliced (about ½ cup)

5 cloves garlic, thinly sliced

¾ teaspoon chili flakes

1 teaspoon smoked paprika

1 teaspoon salt

½ teaspoon freshly ground black pepper

Bring a large pot of salted water to a boil. Roll collard greens into logs, slice into 1-inch strips, and add collards in batches, pushing down to submerge. Cook until tender, 10 minutes.

Transfer collards in a colander. Cool, rinsing under cold water if desired; pat dry.

Heat oil in a large, heavy skillet over medium heat. Add shallots and garlic and cook until fragrant and lightly browned, 2 to 3 minutes.

Add collards, chili flakes, paprika, salt, and pepper and cook, stirring, until collards are wilted, 3 minutes.

Spicy Kale Chips

Makes 6 cups

Kale is one of those crops you can just depend on; it survives a pretty cold, frosty winter and can take a lot of summer heat as well. The first time I tried kale chips, I didn't know what to expect. It was hard to imagine that the moist leaves would turn crunchy and chip-like, but they didn't disappoint. Now they're a part of our family's snack repertoire . . . even kids love them. It's important to make sure the kale is really dry, which helps the chips bake faster and prevents sogginess. You can use the regular, easier-to-find curly kale, but the recipe also works well with Tuscan kale, known in Italy as Nero di Toscana or Cavalo Nero, and State-side as Dinosaur kale because of the way the green leaves resemble a dinosaur's wrinkly skin. Either way, these chips are crispy, crunchy, healthy—and positively addictive. You can vary the seasoning by adding a teaspoon of soy sauce or vinegar to the oil or by introducing a little bit of curry powder into the proceedings.

1 large bunch kale, rinsed and patted dry
1 tablespoon olive oil

1 tablespoon nutritional yeast
¼ teaspoon cayenne pepper

Preheat oven to 325°F.

Trim kale leaves from stems and discard stems. Pat dry an additional time with paper towels or a kitchen towel. Cut into 2-inch pieces. Toss in a bowl with olive oil until evenly coated.

Spread on parchment paper–lined baking sheets, keeping kale pieces separated. Sprinkle with nutritional yeast and cayenne and bake until edges are very lightly browned and "chips" are crispy, 18 to 25 minutes depending on your oven.

Grandma Nellie's Garden Soup

Makes 32 cups

This soup—a family favorite—makes an intentionally large batch; it's meant to be frozen and defrosted whenever a warming bowl of soup is called for. We've come up with a foolproof formula that allows you to mix and match vegetables to your liking, giving you maximum flexibility and ease. If you like your soup sweeter, add more sweet roots. If savory's your thing, take it in that direction with more rutabaga, turnip, and celery root. Herbs, garlic, beans— it's all up to you, making this bubbling pot utterly customizable. The pasta and rice lend a pleasing, almost stew-like thickness. If you want a thinner, all-vegetable soup, simply omit them and take down the water by a cup or two.

1 pound onions, shallots, red onions, or Vidalias, etc.

1 pound chopped carrots, parsnips, rutabaga, or celery root, etc.

1 cup chopped celery

3 cups peeled, chopped potatoes

4 to 5 cups chopped greens (Tuscan kale, chard, spinach, or collards, etc.)

1 pound cubed squash, pumpkin, or sweet potatoes, etc.

12 cups water, plus more if necessary

3 cups canned whole tomatoes in juice or diced tomatoes

1 cup uncooked grains (long-grain rice, rinsed quinoa, barley, or wheat berries, etc.)

2 tablespoons salt

1 teaspoon freshly ground black pepper

3 cloves crushed garlic

6 sprigs fresh herbs (thyme, rosemary, marjoram, etc.), tied with a piece of kitchen twine

1 cup uncooked pasta (any small shape)

2 cups cooked beans (garbanzo, kidney, Hutterite, or Borlotti, etc.)

Combine all ingredients except pasta and beans in a large soup pot and bring to a boil. Reduce heat and simmer, covered until tender and thickened, 3 hours, adding additional water by the cupful if necessary. Add the pasta and beans and cook until tender, an additional 15 minutes.

Remove herb bundle, serve as much soup as you want, then cool soup and freeze in small batches. Soup can be stored in freezer, in airtight containers, for up to 3 months.

Watercress and Water Chestnut–Wonton Soup

Serves 8

Watercress is one of those greens we unfairly relegate to finger sandwiches and other fancy foods. The truth is, it's a versatile green that's packed with antioxidants, vitamin C, vitamin B—and it adds a peppery touch to recipes and salads. At Baker Creek, we harvest two kinds of cress: wild watercress, and leafy sweet-spicy Garden cress. In this savory wonton soup, any of these varieties will work, but Garden cress will be easier to chop. If you can't find any of these, Upland cress or any variety you can find at the farmers' market will do.

Broth
12 cups vegetable stock
1 cup dried mushroom blend

Wontons
1 bunch Garden cress, leaves picked
   (about 4 cups), divided

⅓ cup finely chopped water chestnuts
⅓ cup finely minced chives, divided
3 tablespoons soy sauce, divided
32 4-inch square or round eggless
   wonton skins

Bring stock and mushrooms to a boil. Reduce heat and simmer until mushrooms soften, 15 minutes. Remove from heat and let sit at least 30 minutes or up to 2 hours, to allow broth to infuse with mushroom flavor. Using a slotted spoon, remove ¼ cup mushrooms and finely chop; reserve (leave remaining mushrooms in soup for serving).

Chop 3 cups watercress and combine with water chestnuts, ¼ cup chives, chopped mushrooms, and 1 tablespoon soy sauce in a bowl; reserve.

Place a large piece of parchment paper on a clean, dry work surface. Arrange 16 wonton skins on paper and place 2 teaspoons filling in each wonton. Using a pastry brush, moisten edges of wonton skins with water, then press an additional wonton skin on top and seal with your fingers; cover wontons with a towel until ready to use.

Bring mushroom broth to a simmer and add wontons, reserved 1 cup watercress leaves and remaining 2 tablespoons soy sauce. Simmer until wontons are cooked through, 3 to 4 minutes. Divide among 8 bowls and garnish with remaining chives.

Note: Filled, uncooked wontons can be frozen in a single layer on baking sheets, then transferred to ziplock freezer bags to be used within 1 month.

Little Gem Lettuce Salad with Stone Fruit and Creamy Tarragon Vinaigrette

Serves 4 to 6

Peaches bring back so many memories for me. As a kid, I loved to pick red-fleshed varieties we grew. There were also wild varieties growing on our property that never even got harvested . . . if only I knew then what I know now! These days, new varieties show up on the farm, at the farmers' market—even at the regular grocer's, as is the case with those funny-looking donut peaches originally from China. There's a reason Little Gem lettuce has become such a popular gardeners' and farmers' market choice: The green leaves maintain the integrity of romaine but have the tender softness of butter lettuce. Here, the leaves cradle gorgeous summer stone fruit and a creamy vinaigrette. The fresh tarragon accent coaxes out the very essence of the fruit. Needless to say, you can mix and match the fruit based on what's fresh and available.

Salad

2 heads Little Gem lettuce, rinsed and dried, leaves separated

2 medium heirloom peaches, pitted and cut into wedges

2 medium heirloom plums, such as Mariposas, pitted and cut into wedges

2 tablespoons fresh whole tarragon leaves, plus 2 teaspoons chopped

Dressing

4 tablespoons Vegenaise

2 tablespoons fresh lemon juice

1 teaspoon agave nectar

1 teaspoon Dijon mustard

½ teaspoon salt

¼ teaspoon freshly ground black pepper

Arrange lettuce leaves on a serving platter. Scatter with peach and plum wedges and tarragon leaves.

Whisk together Vegenaise, lemon juice, agave nectar, mustard, salt, pepper, and chopped tarragon and drizzle over salad.

Sweet-and-Sour Walnut-Filled Lettuce Cups

Makes 8 lettuce cups

Lettuce cups are something lots of us find at the local restaurant, but they're just as easy to make at home . . . and more delicious in my estimation. We deep-fry the walnuts for a toasty crunch, but if you like, add them raw to the stir-fried mixture you add to the lettuce "cups." Any butter-, Bibb-, or Boston-style lettuce will suffice, but the reddish hue of Brune D'Hiver lettuce makes for an extra pretty presentation.

1 14.5-ounce block extra-firm tofu, drained	2 tablespoons fresh minced ginger
1 cup plus 2 tablespoons canola oil	4 scallions, greens and whites thinly sliced and kept separate
1 cup shelled walnut halves	½ large red bell pepper, seeded, rinsed, and finely diced
⅓ cup hoisin sauce	
2 tablespoons soy sauce	1 head Butter-type lettuce, such as Brune D'Hiver, Val D'Orges, or May Queen,
2 tablespoons rice vinegar	dark outer leaves saved for another use,
2 teaspoons chili-garlic sauce	inner leaves separated (8 leaves total)
2 teaspoons sesame oil	

Place tofu between two plates and cover top plate with cans or a heavy skillet for about 30 minutes, then drain off extra liquid. Finely mince and reserve.

Heat 1 cup of oil in a small saucepan until very hot but not smoking. Gently lower nuts into skillet and fry until toasted and browned, being careful not to burn, 2 to 3 minutes. Remove and drain on paper towels and reserve.

In a bowl, whisk together hoisin sauce, soy sauce, rice vinegar, chili-garlic sauce, and sesame oil; reserve. Heat remaining 2 tablespoons oil over medium heat in a large sauté pan or wok. Add ginger and scallion whites and cook until whites of onions are translucent and ginger is fragrant, 2 to 3 minutes. Add tofu and cook, stirring, until browned, 4 to 5 minutes. Add reserved sauce, reduce heat to a simmer, and cook, stirring, an additional 3 to 4 minutes. Add fried walnuts and peppers and stir to incorporate. Cook until peppers just begin to soften, an additional minute. Remove mixture from heat.

Fill each lettuce leaf with ⅓ cup filling and top with scallion greens.

Watermelon Syrup

Makes 1½ cups

We've always been intrigued by the idea of natural sweeteners, and here's one to make with your bumper crop of watermelons. Just juice, strain, and boil down to develop a dark pink, syrupy liquid. Use it to sweeten drinks, drizzle on fruit, or as a nice topping on a piece of cake. Of course, you can double or even triple the recipe; you'll just need to increase the simmering time by about 10 minutes per pound of watermelon. For this recipe, pick a deliciously sweet variety like Ali Baba or Charleston Grey.

1 16-pound heirloom watermelon, such as Ali Baba,
    seeds removed and saved for planting

Remove flesh from watermelon rind, reserving rind for another purpose, such as our Pickled Watermelon Rinds (recipe page 108).

Cube flesh. Working in batches, puree watermelon flesh in blender until smooth. Strain twice through a fine-mesh colander, discarding solids each time.

Place juice in a large, heavy saucepan and bring to a boil. Reduce heat and simmer vigorously until strained watermelon juice is thickened and reduced to about 1¼ cups liquid, 4 to 4½ hours, lowering flame when necessary.

Remove from heat, cool completely, and store in an airtight container.

Syrup can be refrigerated in an airtight container for up to 1 month.

Pickled Watermelon Rinds

Makes 3 pints

Don't knock these pickles until you try them! During the summer, with the amount of watermelon we eat, there's always a ton of rind to go around. Rather than discard it, make these sweet-tart pickles. Your sandwiches will never be the same.

1 4-pound piece watermelon

10 cups water, divided, plus more for boiling

3 tablespoons kosher salt

3 cups apple cider vinegar

2½ cups evaporated cane juice crystals

2 teaspoons whole cloves

2 teaspoons pink peppercorns

1 teaspoon whole allspice berries

1 teaspoon whole black peppercorns

1 star anise

1 lime, sliced

3 cinnamon sticks, rinsed

Remove watermelon from rind, and reserve flesh for another use, such as our Watermelon Syrup (recipe page 106); cube rind to yield 8 cups. Combine 8 cups water and salt in a large bowl and add watermelon rind; refrigerate overnight or up to 8 hours. Drain watermelon and rinse three times in cold water.

Place watermelon rind in a large saucepan and cover with fresh water. Bring to a boil, reduce heat, and simmer until almost soft, 15 minutes. Remove from water and drain.

While watermelon is simmering, combine 2 cups water, vinegar, cane juice crystals, cloves, pink peppercorns, allspice, black peppercorns, star anise, and lime in a very large pot. Bring to a boil, reduce heat, and cook over a medium boil until flavors are fused, 15 to 20 minutes. Add watermelon rinds to mixture and simmer until rinds become translucent and flexible, 15 to 20 minutes.

Divide rind among jars and pour liquid over rinds, leaving ½ inch headspace. Add a cinnamon stick to each jar.

Seal jars and process in a water bath canner for 10 minutes. Remove from heat and cool completely before labeling. Check seals after 24 hours, then allow flavors to meld for 2 weeks before opening.

Melon Sorbet

Makes about 3 cups

Until we started making sorbet ourselves, we made do with the store-bought variety. Once you invest in an ice cream maker, you'll never settle for anything less. The flavor of the fruit shines right through, and just the right amount of citrus juice and zest add zingy sunshine to any flavor you choose. Think about making three varieties, then serving them together in small scoops.

1 cup sugar
½ cup water
1 teaspoon finely grated lemon or lime zest

2½ cups cubed sweet-fleshed melon (about 1¼ pound), such as Charentais, Honeydew, or Korean
2 tablespoons lemon or lime juice

Make a simple syrup by combining sugar, water, and citrus zest in a small saucepan and bringing to a boil, stirring to dissolve the sugar. Reduce heat and simmer until clear, 4 to 5 minutes. Remove from heat and cool.

Puree melon, lemon or lime juice, and simple syrup in a food processor until smooth, 30 seconds.

Chill in refrigerator for 4 hours or up to 24 hours. Transfer mixture to an ice cream maker and make according to manufacturer's instructions, until sorbet is slushy and holds its shape, 20 to 25 minutes.

Serve immediately or, for a denser texture, pack into an airtight container and store in freezer up to 1 month.

Icy Melon, Coconut, and Basil Shake

Makes 1 smoothie, about 2½ cups

We hate wasting food at Baker Creek, so we decided to come up with this smoothie using the thinner liquid that remains once you use the coconut cream from the top of a can of coconut milk. I'm always inspired by the food of Southeast Asia, and this shake is based on the refreshing fresh-fruit drinks you'll find all over that region. And since we're known for our melons, this was a great way for us to showcase our just-off-the-vine, in-season fruit. We like the way green melons such as Tam Dew Honeydew, Eden's Gem, or Green Nutmeg look and taste with basil—but any juicy, sweet-fleshed variety will do.

2 cups cubed melon, such as Tam Dew Honeydew, Eden's Gem, or Green Nutmeg

¾ cup skimmed coconut milk*

3 tablespoons water, plus more if necessary

4 large basil leaves

2 teaspoons agave nectar

⅓ teaspoon salt

Combine all ingredients in blender and puree until smooth. Thin with additional coconut milk if necessary.

* Use the liquid that remains after you chill a can of coconut milk and remove the solidified coconut cream for use in Coconut Whipped Cream (recipe page 176). For instant gratification, simply use a light coconut milk or, for a lighter end result, coconut water.

Russian Eggplant and Shiitake Pockets

Makes 16 pockets

The first time I experienced mushroom pockets was at a California Bay Area farmers' market. I loved them so much that Emilee got to work creating her own version. The dough for the recipe was developed from scratch. The first time we made it, we kept our fingers crossed until we realized that it had turned out beautifully. Sometimes in the evenings I'll come home to find Emilee making these, and I'll roll up my sleeves and lend a hand stuffing them before we bake them. They taste delicious straight from the oven, or you can freeze them to bake at a later date for a quick supper when you're short on time.

Dough
2 cups flour, plus more for kneading
¼ teaspoon salt
¼ cup water
½ cup canola oil
½ cup unsweetened almond milk

Filling
2 tablespoons vegetable oil
¾ cup finely diced onion
8 cloves minced garlic
3 Ping Tung eggplants, coarsely chopped
  (about 4 cups)

2 cups sliced shiitake mushroom caps
1½ tablespoons fresh lemon juice
1 teaspoon paprika
¾ teaspoon salt
¼ teaspoon chili flakes
¼ teaspoon freshly ground black pepper
¼ cup chopped fresh parsley
¼ cup thinly sliced fresh basil
1 teaspoon chopped fresh marjoram
2 tablespoons melted coconut oil or
  olive oil

Make dough:
Whisk together flour and salt in a bowl. Form a well in the center of the flour and stir in water, oil, and almond milk with a wooden spoon until incorporated. Transfer to a lightly floured surface and knead until dough is smooth and no longer sticky, 7 to 8 minutes, adding additional flour by the tablespoonful if necessary. Wrap in plastic and let rest at least 30 minutes and up to 1 hour (this is essential for developing a thin, flaky dough).

Make filling:
Heat vegetable oil in a large skillet over medium-high heat. Add onion and cook, stirring,

until translucent, 7 to 8 minutes. Add garlic and cook an additional minute. Add eggplant, mushrooms, lemon juice, paprika, salt, chili flakes, and pepper and cook until eggplant is soft, 7 to 8 minutes. Stir in parsley, basil, and marjoram, remove from heat, and cool.

Fill pockets:

Preheat oven to 425°F. On a lightly floured surface, divide dough into 2 balls and roll each ball into an 8-inch log. Slice each log into 8 pieces and form a round ball out of each piece. Using a rolling pin, roll each ball, one at a time, into a 5- to 6-inch disc, keeping other balls covered with a towel to avoid drying out. Spoon about 3 tablespoons filling in the center of each circle. Fold over filling and press, crimping with a fork as if making a pie shell. Place on a parchment-lined baking sheet and brush generously with melted coconut oil. Bake until lightly browned, 14 to 16 minutes. Serve warm.

Nectarine and Tomato Barbecue Sauce

Makes 4 cups

This silky, fruity sauce can be made with peaches or even plums. We love the way the fruit just lends itself to the flavor and texture of the condiment. It's great on grilled vegetables, sandwiches—even as a dip.

2 large, ripe nectarines (about 1 pound), or 1 pint canned nectarines, drained

2 tablespoons vegetable oil

1 medium onion, chopped (2 cups)

4 cloves garlic, chopped

2 large tomatoes, cored and chopped (about 1 pound)

½ cup apple cider vinegar

¼ cup Vegan Worcestershire Sauce (recipe page 184)

2 teaspoons kosher salt

2 teaspoons freshly ground black pepper

¾ cup dark agave nectar

1 8-ounce can tomato sauce

1 6-ounce can tomato paste

Bring a medium saucepan of water to a boil. Using a paring knife, cut a 1-inch "✕" into the bottom of each nectarine. Drop fruit into boiling water for 30 seconds. Remove with a slotted spoon and drop into an ice water bath. Slip fruit out of skins and chop fruit over a bowl, making sure to reserve juices.

Heat oil in a saucepan over medium-high heat.

Sauté onions, stirring often, until translucent, 7 minutes.

Add garlic and cook an additional minute.

Add nectarines, tomatoes, vinegar, Vegan Worcestershire Sauce, salt, and pepper and bring to a boil. Lower heat to medium and boil until thickened slightly, about 10 minutes.

Add agave nectar, tomato sauce, and tomato paste, return to a boil, and cook, stirring occasionally, until thickened and liquid is reduced by about 2 inches, 20 to 30 minutes. Cool slightly, then blend until smooth. Sauce can be refrigerated in an airtight container for up to 1 month or processed in a water bath canner for 10 minutes for longer storage.

Crispy Oven-Baked Okra Fries with Dukkah Seasoning

Serves 6

Our catalog features an ever-growing collection of interesting, tasty okra cultivars. Okra may have a reputation for sliminess—that signature slipperiness comes from okra's membership in the mallow family, which includes many gelatinous vegetables—but that's a problem that often gets solved if you're using the freshest, smallest okra available. I like stewed okra with tomato sauce, but these oven-baked, crispy okra strips add a whole new dimension to the expected vegetable. Try mixing Hill Country Heirloom Red with a more standard variety like Perkins Long Pod. The Egyptian-inspired dukkah seasoning sprinkled atop adds intrigue here, but it has many other uses as well: mix with olive oil as a great dipper for crusty bread, or toss into salads before dressing with olive oil and lemon.

Okra

1½ pounds very fresh okra

¼ cup extra virgin olive oil

1 teaspoon salt

½ teaspoon freshly ground black pepper

¼ teaspoon cayenne pepper

Dukkah Seasoning

1 cup blanched hazelnuts

½ cup sesame seeds

3 tablespoons coriander seeds

3 tablespoons cumin seeds

2 teaspoons freshly ground black pepper

2 teaspoons Maldon sea salt or other flaky sea salt

1 teaspoon evaporated cane juice crystals

Make okra:

Preheat oven to 425°F.

Using a sharp knife, slice each piece of okra lengthwise into 2 or 4 strips, depending on size of okra. Toss with olive oil, salt, pepper, and cayenne and place on a rimmed baking sheet. Roast, stirring once midway, until crisped and edges are a deep brown, 20 to 25 minutes.

Make dukkah:

Place the hazelnuts on a baking sheet in same oven as okra. Toast, checking often to make sure nuts don't burn, until browned and fragrant, 8 to 10 minutes. Remove from oven and cool completely.

Place sesame seeds in a skillet and toast, tossing often, until toasted and fragrant, 3 to 4 minutes. Turn out onto a plate to cool. Add coriander and cumin seeds to same skillet and toast until fragrant and seeds begin to pop, 1 to 2 minutes. Turn out onto a separate plate and cool.

Grind cumin and coriander in a spice grinder and transfer to a food processor. Add hazelnuts, pepper, salt, and cane juice crystals and pulse until mixture looks like fine sand, being careful not to overprocess nuts, 20 to 25 pulses. Transfer to a bowl and add sesame seeds; you will have almost 2 cups dukkah seasoning.

Assemble dish:

Arrange roasted okra on a platter and sprinkle with 1/3 cup dukkah. Remaining dukkah seasoning can be stored in an airtight container for up to 2 weeks.

Creamy Caramelized Onion Dip

Makes 2½ cups

Chances are, if you look closely at almost any cookbook or explore most world cuisines, there'd be an onion—or something from the onion family—at the heart of many recipes. They come in so many shapes, sizes, and colors, it's fun to mix and match them. Although this recipe calls for a sweet onion such as our Australian Browns, starting with a sharper onion yields great results depending on your taste. This creamy dip develops an almost candy-like sweetness, making for a great contrast on savory sandwiches, with crunchy vegetables, or even swirled into mashed root vegetables or applesauce.

4 tablespoons olive oil
3 exta-large sweet onions, such as Australian Brown (2½ pounds), finely chopped

1 cup soft silken tofu
1 teaspoon salt
½ teaspoon freshly ground black pepper

Heat oil in a large, heavy skillet over medium-high heat.

Add onions and cook, stirring, until onions release their water. Reduce heat and cook onions over low heat, stirring frequently, until caramelized and dark brown, 45 minutes to 1 hour.

Remove from heat and cool to room temperature.

Transfer to a food processor and pulse with tofu, salt, and pepper. Chill and serve with crackers.

Orange and Avocado Summer Rolls with Light Citrus Dipping Sauce

Makes 12 rolls

Traveling in Southeast Asia, you'll see rolls like this everywhere, made with diaphanous rice wrappers that start out hard and brittle but soften as they're soaked in warm water. Rice wrappers take well to all manner of fillings, from tofu and avocado to noodles, apple slices—even cooked yams. Here, carrots and lettuce lend crunch, while avocado and noodles provide a soft landing spot on the palate. The surprise here is a sweet orange segment in the middle, which adds a hit of juiciness at the center of a multitude of contrasting textures and flavors. Accompanying the recipe is my version of a dipping sauce, but feel free to customize it, making it as sweet, spicy, or tangy as you like by playing with the proportions.

6 cups water, plus 1 tablespoon

1 ounce thin Asian rice noodles

4 large leaves red-leaf lettuce, rinsed and patted dry

4 large leaves radicchio

1 large orange

24 8-inch rice wrapper rounds

12 large or 24 small basil leaves

1 medium carrot, cut into 3-inch thin julienne

1 avocado, pitted and thinly sliced

12 large or 24 medium mint leaves

2 tablespoons unseasoned rice wine vinegar

2 tablespoons lime juice

1 tablespoon agave nectar

1 teaspoon No-Fish Fish Sauce (recipe page 179)

1 teaspoon soy sauce

½ teaspoon toasted sesame oil

¼ teaspoon Sriracha or chili paste

Bring 6 cups of water to a boil. Remove from heat and place rice noodles in pot until soft, 10 minutes. Drain in a colander and rinse with cool water; reserve.

Remove spines from lettuce and discard. Trim leaves into 2- x 3-inch squares; reserve, covered with a paper towel.

Trim radicchio leaves into 2- x 3-inch squares; reserve, covered with a paper towel.

Cut ½ inch off of top and bottom of orange to create flat surfaces. Using a sharp knife, cut off skin and rind of orange, working to follow round shape and trying to preserve as much of the orange flesh as possible. Working over a bowl, gently cut between visible membranes to release orange segments, trying hard to keep them whole as you release them. Squeeze excess juice from orange membranes into a bowl, plus any juice that the orange segments released (you should have about 2 tablespoons orange juice).

Clear a large work area and line up all ingredients in bowls.

Fill a clean, large skillet with warm water (replenish with more warm water to maintain temperature as necessary). Arrange a damp clean dish towel on your work surface. Place one rice wrapper round in the skillet and moisten until it begins to soften but is not completely translucent, 30 seconds. Remove from water and place on the damp towel.

Arrange one basil leaf, outer side down, centered about 2½ inches from the edge of the round. Arrange one radicchio piece on top of the basil, followed by 2 lettuce leaves. Top with an orange segment, then 2 tablespoons rice noodles, 1 tablespoon carrots, and 1 slice avocado. Top with a mint leaf. Gently pull bottom of wrapper over filling, then fold in sides as though making a burrito. Roll up and place on a plate lined with a damp paper towel. Cover with another towel and repeat with remaining rolls, leaving space between rolls to prevent sticking.

To make dipping sauce, combine reserved orange juice, rice vinegar, lime juice, agave nectar, remaining tablespoon water, No-Fish Fish Sauce, soy sauce, sesame oil, and Sriracha. Serve with rolls.

Orange-Scented General Tso's Tofu with Romanesco Cauliflower

Serves 6

My love of Asian dishes is no secret. Here, General Tso's chicken gets a vegan twist. We update the Chinese staple by replacing chicken with tofu, and add fresh chunks of orange and orange rind for a citrusy zing. We also use gorgeous, fractal-looking Romanesco cauliflower for a touch of green and fresh-vegetable crunch.

2 14.5-ounce blocks extra-firm tofu

½ cup soft silken tofu

6 tablespoons soy sauce, divided

1 tablespoon water

1 cup cornstarch, divided

Vegetable oil for frying

1 large heirloom orange, plus additional
   slices for garnish

⅔ cup Sweet Thai Chili Sauce
   (recipe page 181)

2 tablespoons rice vinegar

1 tablespoon minced garlic

1 teaspoon Sriracha sauce or other hot
   chili sauce

½ teaspoon chili flakes

1 cup imitation chicken broth, plus more
   if necessary

2 cups lightly steamed Romanesco
   cauliflower florets

Hot jasmine rice for serving

Place each tofu block between two plates and cover each top plate with cans or a heavy skillet for about 30 minutes, draining off extra liquid twice.

Cut each piece of tofu into 16 equal-sized pieces and reserve.

Combine silken tofu, 4 tablespoons soy sauce, water, and ¾ cup cornstarch in a blender and puree until smooth. Transfer to a bowl, add tofu pieces to mixture, and stir to coat; marinate for 5 minutes.

Heat 4 inches vegetable oil in a heavy saucepan to 350°F. Working in batches, fry tofu, stirring to keep pieces from sticking together, until crisp and browned, 3 to 4 minutes, allowing oil to return to ideal heat between batches. Drain on paper towels and keep warm.

Using a vegetable peeler, peel 2 long, inch-wide strips from orange; reserve. Cut off remaining rind and pith and discard, then chop orange into chunks, being sure to reserve juice.

To make the simmering sauce, whisk together orange and reserved juice, 2 strips zest, remaining ¼ cup cornstarch and remaining 2 tablespoons soy sauce, Sweet Thai Chili Sauce, rice vinegar, garlic, Sriracha, chili flakes, and imitation chicken broth in an extra-large, high-sided skillet. Bring to a simmer and cook until slightly thickened, 1 to 2 minutes, thinning slightly with additional broth if necessary.

Add tofu and cauliflower and cook until warmed through, 3 to 4 minutes. Remove orange zest.

Serve with rice and garnish with orange slices.

Lemony Parsnip and Arborio Rice Risotto

Serves 6

Winter means lots of root vegetables, and at Baker Creek, we're always looking for creative ways to use one of our favorites, parsnips. Here, we cut down on the creamy Arborio rice and add tiny bits of diced parsnips, which adds a sweet earthiness to an expected Italian favorite. In a pinch you could use carrots instead of parsnips—or go half and half for more color.

6 cups low-sodium vegetable broth

⅓ cup olive oil, divided, plus more for drizzling

1½ cups finely chopped shallots

1½ pounds parsnips (about 6 medium), peeled, trimmed, and cut into tiny dice

2 tablespoons chopped fresh thyme, plus more for garnish

1 cup Arborio or carnaroli rice

2 tablespoons lemon juice

2 teaspoons finely grated lemon zest

1 tablespoon nutritional yeast

1 teaspoon salt, or to taste

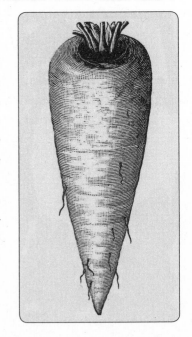

Bring broth to boil in a saucepan, reduce heat, cover, and keep warm on a back burner.

Heat ¼ cup oil in large, heavy saucepan over medium heat. Add shallots and cook, stirring often, until translucent, 5 to 6 minutes. Add parsnips and thyme and cook, stirring, until tender-crisp, 1 to 2 minutes. Add rice and cook, stirring to coat, 1 to 2 minutes. Add 2 cups broth and simmer until almost all broth is absorbed, stirring occasionally, 4 to 5 minutes. Add broth ½ cup at a time and cook, stirring, 1 to 2 minutes after each addition, until mixture absorbs all liquid and rice is just cooked. Stir in lemon juice, lemon zest, nutritional yeast, and salt during last 3 minutes of cooking (after about 15 minutes). Remove from heat; stir in remaining olive oil.

Divide among 6 bowls and garnish with additional thyme and a drizzle of olive oil.

Sunshine Parsnip Muffins

Makes 12 muffins

Carrot muffins? Sure. But parsnip? Less expected. These muffins make a great snack or breakfast on the go, and they're so yummy, you'll want to make them in multiples and freeze them for later. The parsnips make them a little less sweet and wet than their carrot counterparts. Of course, swap in carrots if you don't have parsnips on hand, and be creative: Emilee's mom makes them with the called-for applesauce, but suggests crushed pineapple as a substitute.

2 cups unbleached all-purpose flour
½ cup evaporated cane juice crystals
1 tablespoon baking powder
1 teaspoon salt
1 medium parsnip, finely grated (about 1 cup)
¾ cup coconut milk

½ cup vegetable oil
¼ cup unsweetened applesauce or crushed pineapple
4 teaspoons Ener-G egg replacer, dissolved in 4 tablespoons water
½ cup chopped toasted pecans
1 teaspoon grated orange zest

Preheat oven to 400°F.

Sift together flour, cane juice crystals, baking powder, and salt in a medium-sized bowl.

Combine parsnips, coconut milk, oil, applesauce, and reconstituted egg replacer in another bowl; fold in pecans and orange zest.

Add dry ingredients to wet ingredients and combine until moistened.

Grease a 12-compartment muffin tin and spoon about ⅓ cup batter in each compartment.

Bake until a toothpick inserted in center comes out clean, 25 to 30 minutes. Transfer to a wire rack and cool completely.

Smashed Parsnips and Turnips with Roasted Garlic Scapes

Serves 8, makes 6½ cups

We're asking you to reconsider the lowly root vegetable. When it gets difficult to even look at another potato, recipes like this can help vary your kitchen repertoire. Here, the bitterness of turnips (try anything from purple-topped White Globe or Ideal Purple to milder imported Boule D'Or) contrasts with the sweetness of the parsnips. They both get boiled and mashed with the surprise of late-summer garlic scapes, those whimsical garlic-plant tops that combine a familiar flavor with an unfamiliar package.

1 cup (about 4 ounces) garlic scapes

2 tablespoons olive oil

1½ teaspoons salt, divided

1 teaspoon freshly ground black pepper, divided

2 pounds parsnips, peeled and cut unto 2-inch cubes

2 pounds turnips, peeled and cut into 2-inch cubes

4 cups vegetable stock

2 cups water

½ cup unsweetened soymilk

1 vegan buttery stick, such as Earth Balance, or ½ cup olive oil

Preheat oven to 450°F. Toss garlic scapes in a bowl with oil, ½ teaspoon salt, and ½ teaspoon pepper and spread on a cookie sheet. Cover with foil and roast until edges are caramelized and scapes are soft, about 30 minutes. Remove from oven, cool, and chop.

Combine parsnips, turnips, stock, and water in a pot and bring to a boil. Reduce heat and cook, simmering, until vegetables are tender, 30 minutes; drain, reserving 1 cup cooking liquid.

Return to pot and combine with chopped scapes, soymilk, buttery stick, and remaining salt and pepper, adding reserved cooking liquid to thin if necessary.

Green Pea Falafel with Tahini Sauce

Serves 6

When most people think falafel, they think chickpeas. While I love the traditional version, I'm also a fan of this newfangled falafel, which uses sweet shelled summer peas instead of the more floury chickpeas. While our version uses parsley and cilantro for an herb counterpoint, feel free to swap in mint or even tarragon as part of the mix. We also added bread crumbs, which help compensate for the extra moisture.

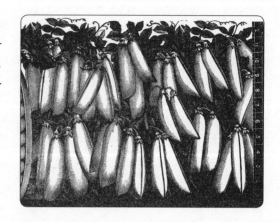

Falafel

2 cups fresh or frozen peas

3 tablespoons fresh vegan bread crumbs

1 tablespoon flour

2 cloves smashed garlic

⅓ cup chopped parsley

⅓ cup chopped cilantro

1 teaspoon salt

¾ teaspoon ground cumin

½ teaspoon freshly ground black pepper

½ teaspoon baking soda

½ teaspoon baking powder

¼ teaspoon ground coriander

Tahini Sauce

½ cup Homemade Tahini (recipe page 178)

2 cloves garlic

½ teaspoon kosher salt

2 tablespoons olive oil

3 to 4 tablespoons lemon juice

1 teaspoon chopped parsley

Pita bread, chopped tomatoes, and cucumbers for serving

Make falafel:

If using frozen peas, defrost peas completely, then place in a preheated skillet for 2 minutes to release more liquid; drain. If using fresh peas, blanch peas in boiling hot water for 3 minutes, then drain and reserve.

Pulse all falafel ingredients in a food processor until almost smooth, but a few chunks of peas remain, 15 to 20 pulses. Form generous tablespoons of batter into walnut-sized balls (batter will make 20 to 24 balls).

Heat 3 inches of oil to 350°F in a deep fryer or heavy saucepan. Working in batches of 3 or 4, gently drop balls into oil and fry until dark brown on the outside, 3 to 4 minutes. Remove from oil and drain on paper towels.

Make tahini sauce:
Whisk together Homemade Tahini, garlic, salt, olive oil, lemon juice, and parsley.

Assemble:
Serve falafel in pita bread with chopped tomatoes, cucumbers, and tahini sauce.

Basmati Rice with Saffron and Peas

Serves 8

Shelling peas on our front porch was a childhood ritual. Mom and Grandma would sit on the porch extracting the peas from their pods until a four-foot pile of shells—taller than I was at the time—developed. I would often find myself snacking on the peas as we went along, but Mom and Grandma never seemed to mind.

3 cups low-sodium imitation chicken-
　flavored broth, or water
¼ teaspoon saffron threads
3 tablespoons safflower oil
1 medium onion, diced (1½ cups)
2 cups white basmati rice

1½ cups fresh shelled Wando, Tall
　Telephone, or Lincoln peas, or frozen
　green peas
Salt and freshly ground black pepper to
　taste

In a saucepan, heat broth until very hot but not boiling. With your fingers, crush saffron threads, add to broth, and set aside to steep.

Heat oil over medium-high heat. Add onion and cook until onion soft and translucent, 7 to 8 minutes. Add rice and cook, stirring often, until rice starts to brown, an additional 2 to 3 minutes. Add saffron broth to rice, bring to a boil, reduce heat, and simmer, tightly covered, until rice is almost cooked, 15 to 16 minutes.

Remove lid and add peas; do not stir. Cover and continue cooking for an additional 4 minutes. Remove pot from heat, let stand 5 minutes, then fluff with a fork. Season with salt and pepper to taste.

African Peanut Soup

Makes 12 cups

This soup is yet another use for sweet potatoes, butternut squash, or pumpkin. It also uses natural-style peanut butter for a creamy soup indigenous to African countries, where peanuts are a staple crop and a major source of nutrition and sustenance.

2 tablespoons coconut oil

1 large onion, chopped

1 very large or 2 medium Beauregard sweet potatoes (1 pound), cubed (2½ cups)

4 cloves garlic, chopped

1 tablespoon minced ginger

½ teaspoon chili flakes

4 cups vegetable stock

1 14.5-ounce can diced tomatoes in juice

¾ cup creamy natural-style peanut butter

1 teaspoon salt

¼ cup chopped toasted peanuts

Cilantro leaves for garnish

Heat oil in a medium saucepan over medium-high heat. Add onions and sweet potatoes and cook until onions are translucent and sweet potatoes begin to soften, 5 to 6 minutes. Add garlic, ginger, and chili flakes, and cook, stirring, an additional 3 to 4 minutes. Add vegetable stock, tomatoes, peanut butter, and salt, bring to boil, reduce heat, and cook until sweet potatoes are tender, an additional 10 minutes. Remove from heat and cool slightly, then puree in batches in the blender. Divide among bowls, and garnish with peanuts and cilantro.

Savory Black-Eyed Peas

Makes 5 cups

Along with watermelon and okra, these black-dotted beans—also known as cowpeas—were brought over by African slaves hundreds of years ago. I became more interested in them once I came to Missouri and they found fertile ground to flourish on our property. Most garden peas don't do well in the South, but the cowpea is a species that thrives in hot weather and is a staple of Southern cuisine. They have an earthy, nutty flavor profile and are incredibly versatile. They can be served in so many different ways: steamed, baked, or stewed among them. My favorites are Purple Hill Pink Eye—they're earthy and have a mineral-like taste on the tongue. When the peas inside aren't totally mature, you can snap the pods open, steam the peas with some garlic and salt, and they make for excellent eating. Since fresh black-eyed peas are very hard to find in most of the country, we offer this recipe using dried.

1½ cups dried black-eyed peas

2 tablespoons olive oil

1 medium onion, chopped (about 1½ cups)

3 cloves crushed garlic

1 cup chopped celery

1 teaspoon dried oregano

½ teaspoon dried basil

2 whole dried chiles de arbol

1 26-ounce can diced tomatoes in juice

2 large bay leaves

½ teaspoon liquid smoke or smoked paprika

½ teaspoon salt

½ teaspoon freshly ground black pepper

Place peas in a bowl and cover with cold water. Soak at least 8 hours or up to 16. Drain water from peas, place in a medium saucepan, cover with four inches of fresh water, and bring to a boil. Reduce heat and simmer until beans are tender, 25 to 35 minutes (depending on how long you soaked the beans). Drain and cool.

Heat oil in a large, heavy skillet over medium heat and cook onions, stirring, until lightly browned, 9 to 10 minutes. Add garlic and cook an additional minute, then add celery and cook until tender-crisp, an additional 3 minutes.

Stir in oregano, basil, and chiles, being careful not to break chiles. Add diced tomatoes, bring to a boil, reduce heat, and simmer, stirring, for 5 minutes. Add cooked peas, bay leaves, liquid smoke, salt, and pepper, return to a boil, reduce heat, and simmer until peas absorb most of the tomato liquid, 15 to 20 minutes. Remove dried chiles and bay leaves and serve.

Muscadine Poached Pears

Serves 8

We love to visit North Carolina in the late summer, when Muscadine grapes are ripe. From the fruit itself to pressed Muscadine cider, once you've experienced their dusky-sweet flavor you're bound to be hooked on this Southern variety. We take inspiration from the delicious Muscadine elixir here, using it to poach tiny seasonal pears in a spice-laden liquid that imparts the perfect flavor balance to the gorgeous ripe fruit. Just make sure not to throw away the poaching liquid—dilute it with a bit of water for a most glorious beverage.

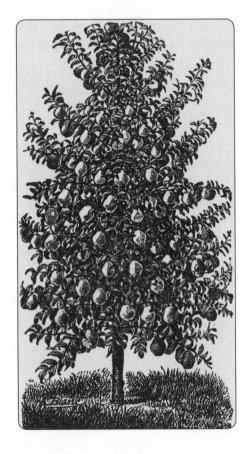

5½ cups Muscadine grape cider or white
　　grape juice
4½ cups water
½ cup amber agave nectar
1 vanilla bean, split
1 teaspoon minced fresh ginger
2 teaspoons whole cloves
1 cinnamon stick
16 small pears, such as Forel or Seckel

Combine all ingredients, except for pears, in a stockpot, and bring to a gentle boil.

Carefully peel pears, leaving the stems intact, and place in hot liquid.

Cook, simmering, just until pears are fork-tender, about 20 minutes. Remove from heat and cool in poaching liquid. Serve pears in bowls or parfait glasses with poaching liquid.

Grilled Baby Peppers with Muhamarra Sauce

Serves 8

We love all kinds of peppers here at Baker Creek, but the mini peppers in our annual catalog are some of the most sought-after varieties. Grilling them whole makes them into tiny charred bundles that take to sauces with ease. This walnut-infused Turkish muhamarra dip calls for regular bell peppers. Any variety from your garden or farmers' market will do just fine, though deep, dark Sweet Chocolate peppers would add color intrigue as well as a touch of extra sweetness to contrast with the tang of the muhamarra dip's pomegranate molasses, a condiment you can find at Middle Eastern grocers and specialty markets. The muhamarra can also be used as a dip with crudités or pita chips.

Muhamarra Sauce (makes 2 cups)

3 large Golden or Red Marconi peppers (about 1¼ pounds)

1¼ cups walnuts, lightly toasted

½ cup vegan bread crumbs

1 tablespoon pomegranate molasses

1 tablespoon fresh lemon juice

1 teaspoon ground cumin

¼ teaspoon cayenne pepper

3 tablespoons extra virgin olive oil, plus more if necessary

Peppers

1 pound Sweet Yellow Stuffing mini bell peppers or other mini bell peppers

1 pound Sweet Red Stuffing mini bell peppers or other mini bell peppers

1 tablespoon olive oil

½ teaspoon salt

¼ teaspoon freshly ground black pepper

Make muhamarra:

Preheat oven to 525°F.

Place bell peppers on a baking sheet and roast, turning once, until puffed and blackened on exterior, 30 to 35 minutes.

Remove from oven. Using tongs, carefully transfer peppers to a heatproof container and cover tightly; cool for 30 minutes. Remove from container, drain and discard any excess liquid, and remove and discard seeds and peels from peppers.

Combine peppers, walnuts, bread crumbs, pomegranate molasses, lemon juice, cumin, and cayenne in a food processor and pulse 30 times until chunky. With the motor running, add oil in a slow stream until mixture forms a smooth paste, adding additional oil if necessary. Transfer to an airtight container and reserve. Muhamarra will keep in refrigerator in an airtight container for up to 1 week.

Grill peppers:

Preheat a grill or grill pan over medium-high heat.

Toss oil, salt, and pepper in a large mixing bowl to coat.

Grill peppers until grill marks form and peppers begin to slump, 5 minutes per side. Remove from grill, arrange on a plate, and serve with muhamarra sauce.

Pepper Hot Sauce

Makes 4 cups

Anyone who knows hot peppers knows that once they start growing, you almost can't stop them! This is a great way to use up extra peppers. If you find any of these sauces too overbearingly hot, you can add some roasted sweet bell pepper to the sauce. Making this sauce can be a literal tear-jerker, so use gloves to chop the peppers, and keep your workspace well-ventilated.

1 pound hot peppers of your choice
   (serranos, Anaheims, jalapeños, etc.)
1½ cups white vinegar
8 garlic cloves

1 teaspoon salt
1 roasted, seeded red, green, or yellow
   bell pepper (optional)

Chop stems off peppers, then roughly chop peppers. Bring vinegar to a vigorous simmer, then add peppers, lower heat, and cook over a very low flame until peppers are tender, 8 to 10 minutes. Remove from heat and carefully strain peppers from liquid, reserving liquid. Carefully place peppers in blender, then ladle in ½ cup strained liquid. Add garlic and salt, cover, and blend until smooth, 30 seconds. Add additional liquid by the tablespoonful to achieve desired consistency. If pepper sauce is too spicy for your taste, blend in optional roasted pepper. Transfer to an airtight container and store in refrigerator.

Without addition of bell peppers, Pepper Hot Sauce will keep, covered in an airtight container, in refrigerator for up to 2 months. With bell peppers, sauce will keep for 2 weeks.

Cabbage-Stuffed Mini Peppers

Makes 3 quart-sized jars

We adapted this recipe from an Amish friend who sells these peppers at her local produce auction. One of her secrets is placing a small wedge of pineapple on each cabbage-stuffed pepper to prevent the cabbage from floating upward during canning. It works like a charm, looks pretty, and flavors the brine with a delicious tropical note.

1 pineapple, rind removed

2½ pounds multicolored Baby Bell or Mini Stuffing peppers

3½ cups sugar

2 cups white vinegar

1 cup water

1½ teaspoons non-iodized salt

3 cups finely shredded white cabbage

Cut three ½-inch-thick discs from pineapple; reserve remaining pineapple for another use. Using the size of the peppers as your guide, cut a piece from each pineapple disc that will fit tightly when stuffed into the top of each pepper; reserve pieces.

Combine sugar, vinegar, water, and salt in a saucepan, bring to a boil, and simmer until sugar is dissolved, 3 to 4 minutes. Cover and keep hot over a low flame.

Remove stems from tops of peppers, remove seeds, and rinse peppers.

Using clean hands, pack peppers tightly with cabbage, leaving about an inch on the top of each pepper. Stuff peppers with pineapple so pieces are packed in tight on top of shredded cabbage. Arrange stuffed peppers as close together as possible in 3 sterilized quart-sized jars.

Fill jars with liquid, pouring carefully between peppers so as not to dislodge any loose cabbage (some cabbage may float to top of jar—not to worry!). Remove air bubbles with a knife or spatula.

Seal and process in a water bath canner for 10 minutes.

Remove from heat and cool completely before labeling.

Store peppers for 2 weeks before serving to allow flavors to meld.

Persimmon-Pecan-Cherry Chunk Cookies

Makes 3 dozen

My mother made persimmon cookies with ripe fruit late October through early November. Persimmons grow wild in the Ozark Mountains, and there's hardly a prettier sight than their hue seen hanging through barren trees. After the first frost, persimmons turn delightfully sweet, making them perfect for this cookie. If you don't have access to the wild variety, most grocers carry in-season Hachiya persimmons. You know they're ripe when the flesh is juicy and fragrant—just make sure to buy an extra few for eating out of a hand. If you want to make these more indulgent, swap out the dried fruit for chocolate chips.

3 ripe Hachiya persimmons (about ¾ pound), peeled

2 tablespoons flaxseed meal

½ teaspoon cinnamon

½ teaspoon ginger

¼ teaspoon allspice

1 tablespoon vanilla

⅔ cup vegan buttery stick, melted and cooled

1¼ cups packed organic brown sugar

¾ cup light coconut milk

1 cup whole wheat pastry flour

1 teaspoon baking soda

½ teaspoon salt

1 cup chopped pecans

1 cup dried tart cherries

Preheat oven to 375°F.

Mash persimmons with a fork until chunky (do not puree) and place in a large bowl (you should have about 1 cup mash).

Add flaxseed meal, cinnamon, ginger, allspice, and vanilla, then stir in buttery stick, brown sugar, and coconut milk. Whisk together flour, baking soda, and salt and add ½ cup at a time until a stiff batter forms, then gently fold in pecans and cherries.

Drop batter 1 tablespoon at a time onto parchment-lined baking sheets, leaving 2 inches between cookies. Bake until edges are golden and centers are still soft, 15 to 18 minutes. After 5 minutes, transfer to a rack and cool completely.

Old-Fashioned Heirloom Potato Salad

Serves 8 to 10

My sister, Jessica, recommends using two colors of potatoes to make this salad extra special. When picking potatoes for this recipe, try to find ones that are close in size for easy cooking. Look for firm Peruvian blues, with their deep-purple hue and slightly waxy texture, and buttery yellow Yukon Golds.

Salad

3 pounds medium-sized Yukon Gold potatoes

2 pounds medium-sized Peruvian blue potatoes

2 stalks celery, trimmed and finely diced (1 cup)

½ cup finely diced red onion

¼ cup chopped chives, plus more for garnish

Dressing

1½ cups Vegenaise

½ cup sweet pickle relish or Zucchini Relish (recipe page 170)

⅔ cup drained pickled cocktail onions, thinly sliced

2 tablespoons freshly squeezed lemon juice

1 tablespoon chopped fresh dill

2 teaspoons kosher salt

¾ teaspoon freshly ground black pepper

½ teaspoon smoked paprika

Prepare salad:

Place potatoes in a heavy stockpot, cover with cold water, and bring to a rolling boil. Reduce heat to medium-high and gently boil until potatoes are fork tender, 25 to 30 minutes. Drain in

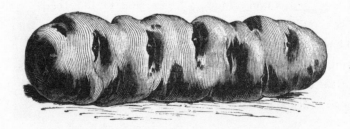

a colander, cool, and refrigerate potatoes until completely chilled, at least 3 hours, or over-night. Peel potatoes and cut into ½-inch pieces.

Place in large mixing bowl and add celery, red onion, and chives.

Make dressing:

Whisk together Vegenaise, pickle relish, cocktail onion, lemon juice, dill, salt, pepper, and smoked paprika.

Finish salad:

Pour dressing over salad and gently stir until well coated.

Chill at least 4 hours or overnight. Transfer to a serving bowl and garnish with additional chives.

Old-Fashioned Potato Kugel

Serves 12

The word "kugel" means "round" in German, and probably refers to the shape of the original dish used to bake a whole variety of casseroles. This potato pudding couldn't be more basic... or more delicious. If you can find one, an old-fashioned safety grater (available at most kitchen and housewares stores) is essential to achieving the desired consistency, which is somewhere between a pudding and a soufflé. Don't be scared off by the two-hour baking time; it's essential to both the crispy exterior and the melt-in-your-mouth center.

1 cup silken tofu
1½ tablespoons Ener-G egg
   replacer, dissolved in 6 tablespoons
   water

5 pounds Eastern, Idaho, or russet
   potatoes
3 to 4 tablespoons vegetable oil
1 tablespoon kosher salt

Place tofu and reconstituted egg replacer in blender and puree until smooth; reserve. Peel potatoes and submerge in cold water to prevent discoloration.

Preheat oven to 350°F. Add oil to a glass 9- x 13-inch pan and heat pan in oven until oil is very hot but not smoking, 10 minutes.

Remove potatoes from water and grate into a large bowl and discard most liquid. Add tofu mixture and salt and stir until incorporated.

Open oven, remove pan, and gently pour batter into hot pan (hot oil will rise up to the edges).

Using a spoon, swirl hot oil over top of potato mixture.

Quickly return pan to oven and bake until bottom, edges, and top are a deep golden brown, about 2 hours. Serve immediately.

Breakfast Hash

Serves 6

This is the kind of recipe that my sister, Jessica, and I might have enjoyed for breakfast when we shared a house together at Baker Creek. While I specialize in more exotic recipes used to experiment with the diverse flavors growing in our gardens, Jessica—a great cook in her own right—is known more for her home-style meals, which she has served to many a lucky houseguest.

2 large Idaho potatoes (about 1 pound)
6 tablespoons olive oil, divided
1 cup finely diced onion
1 small green bell pepper, seeded and diced
2 cloves crushed garlic
1 cup cold cooked brown rice

3 tablespoons nutritional yeast flakes
2 tablespoons chopped fresh parsley, plus more for garnish
1 tablespoon unbleached all-purpose flour
½ teaspoon salt
½ teaspoon freshly ground black pepper

Cover potatoes with water in a large saucepan and bring to a boil. Reduce heat and simmer vigorously until potatoes are just tender, 20 to 25 minutes. Remove from heat, drain, and cool in a large bowl. Shred on a box grater and reserve.

While potatoes are boiling, heat 2 tablespoons oil in a cast-iron skillet over medium-high heat. Add onions, peppers, and garlic and cook, stirring occasionally, until onions are golden and peppers are softened, 10 to 12 minutes. Remove from heat.

Add onion mixture to potatoes, then add rice, nutritional yeast, parsley, flour, salt, and pepper. Stir to incorporate.

Heat remaining oil in a well-

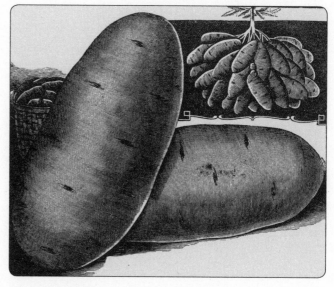

seasoned cast-iron or nonstick skillet over medium heat. Spread hash mixture over hot oil and cook, without flipping or moving, until underside is very dark and crisp but not burned, 10 to 15 minutes. Break up hash and continue to cook until hash continues to brown, an additional 5 to 10 minutes. Remove from heat. Serve hot with Pepper Hot Sauce (recipe page 133), Soy Sour Cream (recipe page 180), and additional chopped parsley.

Sweet Potato Casserole

Serves 8

We like to take this dish with us to family gatherings and holiday meals since our whole family loves sweet potatoes. They grow exceptionally well in our gardens and are one of the crowning jewels to be harvested each season. Not only are they delicious, but they store easily, making them a must-have for the winter months. This recipe actually calls for Garnet yams. Most Americans think of yams as tubers with gorgeous bright-orange flesh, but there are also versions with paler skin and flesh. There's another important point of distinction: the difference between sweet potatoes and yams. True yams, which originally hail from Africa, come in many shapes and sizes. The ones sold in stores stateside are often labeled and look like yams, but they are really sweet potatoes. While it's important to know the difference, most vital is choosing a variety that cooks up sweet, creamy, and not too fibrous—one reason we love luscious Garnet yams.

Casserole

4 large Garnet yams (3 pounds), scrubbed and dried

½ cup (1 stick) vegan buttery stick, such as Earth Balance or coconut oil

4 teaspoons Ener-G egg replacer, dissolved in 4 tablespoons warm water

½ cup turbinado sugar or Sucanat crystals

1 tablespoon vanilla

½ teaspoon salt

½ teaspoon cinnamon

Topping

⅔ cup brown sugar

5 tablespoons unbleached all-purpose flour

⅔ cup chopped pecans

¼ cup (½ stick) vegan buttery stick, such as Earth Balance, cut into small cubes and frozen

Prepare casserole:

Preheat oven to 350°F.

Prick yams with a fork, wrap individually in foil, and place on a cookie sheet. Bake until tender, 60 to 70 minutes.

Remove from oven and cool in foil. Remove and discard skins and mash sweet potatoes in a bowl (you should have about 6 cups sweet potatoes). While still warm, add buttery stick, reconstituted egg replacer, sugar, vanilla, salt, and cinnamon, and whip with a hand mixer until fluffy, 1 to 2 minutes. Transfer to a greased 8- x 8-inch glass baking dish.

Make topping:

Combine brown sugar, flour, and pecans in a medium-sized bowl. Cut in buttery stick with two knives until a chunky, crumbly topping is formed.

Finish casserole:

Sprinkle topping evenly over sweet potato mixture and bake until heated through and topping is lightly browned, 55 to 60 minutes.

Daikon Radish Cakes with Mizuna and Mushrooms

Makes 24 two-inch squares

Glutinous, crispy-edged snacks like this typically contain dried shrimp and bacon; this is our vegan version featuring shiitake mushrooms, tempeh bacon, and mizuna, a green most often served raw. Though almost always called turnip cakes, these snacks actually use a Chinese radish easily replaced with daikon radish for the main ingredient. Rice flour binds the steamed radish and vegetables together, and a proper steam brings the whole dish together. Once they're cooked, pan-frying is essential to add crunch and texture. Serve as a snack, or dole out larger portions with a dressed mizuna salad for a light lunch.

1 large (1¼ pound) Miyashige or Japanese Minowase Daikon radish, peeled and finely shredded (about 8 cups)

2 cups mizuna greens (arugula may be substituted)

2 tablespoons canola oil, divided, plus additional oil for frying

½ pound Shiitake mushroom caps, thinly sliced (about 4 cups)

½ (4 to 5 strips) of a 6-ounce package tempeh "bacon," crumbled

3 cups rice flour

1½ cups water

2 teaspoons salt

1 tablespoon rice vinegar

1 tablespoon agave nectar

Soy sauce for garnish

Place shredded radish in a small-holed steamer basket and steam until radish is soft and translucent, 30 minutes. Remove from heat and cool.

Fill a small saucepan with water and bring to a boil. Add mizuna and cook until wilted, 1 to 2 minutes. Drain in a colander. When cool enough, squeeze excess liquid from greens, chop, and reserve.

Heat 1 tablespoon oil in a heavy skillet over medium-high heat. Add mushrooms and cook until they have released their water and begin to crisp, 5 to 6 minutes; remove and reserve. Add an additional tablespoon oil, then add tempeh bacon and cook, stirring, until crisp, 5 to 6 minutes. Combine with mushrooms and reserve.

Stir together rice flour, water, and salt until well combined. Combine with cooled daikon, cooked mushrooms, and tempeh bacon, mizuna, rice vinegar, and agave nectar, and transfer to a greased 9- x 13-inch-metal pan, smoothing surface with a spatula. Place a baker's cooling rack or an inverted half-quarter-sheet pan inside a large, high-sided roasting pan and place prepared pan on top of rack. Carefully fill roasting pan with two inches boiling water to create a steam environment. Cover roasting pan tightly with aluminum foil and steam on stovetop over medium-low heat until firm, about 1 hour, checking water level and adding more hot water as necessary to keep steam circulating.

Remove from heat and cool on counter for 1 hour. Cut into 24 equal-sized squares.

Heat 1 tablespoon oil in a large skillet over medium-high heat. Add squares in batches and fry until crisp, 1 to 2 minutes per side, adding more oil by the tablespoon as necessary. Serve immediately with soy sauce or other Asian condiments of your choice.

Cold Three-Radish and Rice Noodle Salad

Serves 6

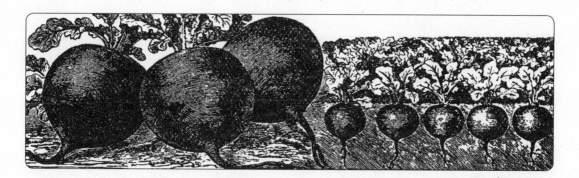

Radishes can run the gamut from sweet to spicy, something evident in this recipe, where you can choose from any varieties you have and taste the difference between spicy black, mellow Daikon, sweet Helios, and mildly assertive French Breakfasts. The chewy rice noodles provide a textural counterpart, and a slick, nutty-salty dressing completes the picture. You can make the salad in advance, but I think it tastes best if dressed just before serving.

¾ pound thick Thai rice sticks

2 tablespoons toasted sesame oil, divided

2 tablespoons soy sauce, plus more to taste

2 teaspoons seasoned rice vinegar

1 teaspoon Sriracha sauce or chili sauce

2 cups assorted sliced radishes, such as Black Spanish, Helios, Watermelon, French Breakfast, or Daikon

1 cup chopped scallions, greens and whites

½ small Asian pear cut, into matchsticks

½ cup chopped cilantro

Bring a large pot of salted boiling water to a boil. Add rice sticks and cook, stirring, until tender-firm, 5 to 6 minutes. Transfer to a colander and rinse well with cold water; drain as much as possible, then transfer to a bowl and toss with 1 teaspoon of the sesame oil to prevent noodles from sticking; chill noodles for 15 to 20 minutes. Whisk together remaining sesame oil, soy sauce, rice vinegar, and Sriracha. Add dressing to noodles and toss with radishes, scallions, Asian pear, and cilantro. Season with additional soy sauce, if desired.

Rhubarb-Strawberry Soup with Basil and Balsamic Vinegar

Serves 6

We've all had strawberry soup, but adding rhubarb intensifies the pink hue and flavor intrigue of this dish, which can be served as a first course, dessert, or snack. I love the way the vegetal quality of the basil plays off the floral fruitiness of the berries and the sweetened rhubarb, while the balsamic and peppercorns add elegance.

1¼ pounds rhubarb stalks, trimmed and chopped (5 cups)

3½ cups water

½ pound strawberries, sliced (1½ cups), plus more for garnish

½ cup agave nectar

¼ teaspoon salt

1 tablespoon aged balsamic vinegar (optional)

2 tablespoons chopped fresh basil

1 teaspoon cracked pink peppercorns for garnish (optional)

Bring rhubarb and water to a boil in a large saucepan. Cook until the rhubarb is soft, 5 minutes. Transfer to a medium bowl. Refrigerate, loosely covered, stirring occasionally, until cool, 1 hour.

Transfer rhubarb to a blender. Add strawberries, agave nectar, and salt and blend until smooth. Transfer to a bowl and refrigerate for 1 hour.

Ladle soup into 6 bowls and drizzle each with ½ teaspoon balsamic vinegar. Sprinkle with chopped basil and pink peppercorns.

Rhubarb Crisp

Serves 6 to 8

According to the wonderful book *Vegetables from Amaranth to Zucchini* by Elizabeth Schneider, rhubarb—which hails from China and Siberia—started as a purely medicinal crop. Technically a vegetable, it gets more play as a fruit since it plays so well with sugar. Use either greenish Victoria or the less-bitter Glaskins Perpetual for this crumble, which has a great, sweet crunchy topping thanks to toasted walnuts.

Filling

1 cup evaporated cane juice crystals

3 tablespoons cornstarch

2 pounds rhubarb, trimmed and cut into ¾-inch pieces (about 6 cups)

Juice and zest of 1 orange

Topping

½ cup unbleached all-purpose flour

½ cup whole wheat pastry flour

¾ cup evaporated cane juice crystals

½ cup brown sugar

½ teaspoon salt

1½ sticks (12 tablespoons) very cold vegan buttery sticks, such as Earth Balance, or ¾ cup chilled coconut shortening, cut into ½-inch cubes

½ cup chopped walnuts

Make filling:

Preheat oven to 375°F. Whisk together cane juice crystals, brown sugar, and cornstarch in a large bowl. Fold in rhubarb and toss to coat, than add orange juice and zest. Transfer to a 3-quart greased casserole dish.

Make topping:

Place flours, cane juice crystals, brown sugar, and salt in the bowl of a food processor and pulse 5 times to incorporate (or whisk by hand in a large bowl).

Add buttery stick and pulse until mixture forms clumps with some pea-sized pieces (or cut buttery sticks in using two knives or a pastry cutter). Transfer to a bowl, fold in walnuts, and sprinkle topping over rhubarb.

Place dish on a rimmed baking sheet to prevent dripping and bake until filling is bubbly and topping is browned, 60 to 65 minutes. Remove from oven, cool slightly, and serve with Strawberry Ice Cream (recipe page 46).

Rhubarb Limeade

Makes 6 cups

This pink syrup looks sweet and simple but has a hint of rhubarb's tongue-twisting tartness. In a pinch it can work as a drizzle over fruit salad, or even heated with hot water to make a kind of sweet hot tea.

1 pound rhubarb stalks (about 8), trimmed and chopped (4 cups)

1½ cups water

1 cup light agave nectar

4 ½- x 3-inch strips lime peel (from 1 lime)

⅔ cup fresh lime juice

4 cups water

Bring rhubarb, water, agave nectar, and lime peel to a boil in a medium saucepan. Reduce heat and simmer until tender, 5 minutes. Pour over a fine-mesh strainer and press down with a wooden spoon to release all liquid; discard solids. Cool completely (makes about 2¼ cups syrup).

Combine 1¼ cups rhubarb syrup, lime juice, and water in a pitcher and chill. Serve in ice-filled glasses garnished with lime wedges.

Thick Lentil Soup with Salsify, Kale, and Smoked Tofu

Serves 8 to 10

If you need a great pot of soup to get you through the week, this one will do the trick. It's packed with nutritious vegetables and lentils, and it's also got a surprise ingredient: salsify. This gnarly root is said to taste like oysters or artichokes, but I think it has a flavor all its own. It's great roasted or fried, and also as a fiber-rich addition to one-pot meals. This soup freezes well; if you can't find salsify, use parsnips. And if you like a creamier soup, take a stick blender to the pot and puree to your liking, leaving some smooth and some chunkier.

2 tablespoons canola oil

1 large onion, chopped (2 cups)

3 cloves minced garlic

1 salsify root, peeled and chopped (1 cup)

2 stalks celery, chopped (1 cup)

1 large carrot, chopped

1 pound green lentils, picked through

1 8-ounce package smoked tofu, diced

12 cups imitation low-sodium chicken broth, plus more if necessary

2 teaspoons salt

½ teaspoon fresh ground pepper

1 teaspoon dried basil

1 teaspoon dried thyme

1 bunch red kale (about ¾ pound), chopped

Heat oil in a large soup pot over medium-high heat.
Add onion and cook until translucent, 5 to 6 minutes.
Add garlic and cook an additional minute.
Add salsify, celery, and carrots and cook until vegetables are softened, 5 to 6 minutes.
Add lentils, tofu, broth, salt, pepper, basil, and thyme and bring to a boil. Reduce heat, add kale, and cook until lentils are tender, 40 to 45 minutes, adding additional broth if necessary.

Spinach and Sesame Bundles

Makes 6 bundles

Got a lot of basil? If you're growing it, chances are you probably do. These flavorful bundles benefit from the addition of basil leaves to the more expected spinach. Both greens wilt in hot water, then get cooled and formed into round little discs lavished with a salty-sweet, tahini-rich dressing. A sprinkling of sesame seeds on top completes the package.

2 tablespoons Homemade Tahini
   (recipe page 178)
1 tablespoon soy sauce
1 teaspoon agave nectar

1½ pounds baby spinach leaves
   (about 12 cups)
3 cups basil leaves, rinsed
2 teaspoons lightly toasted sesame seeds

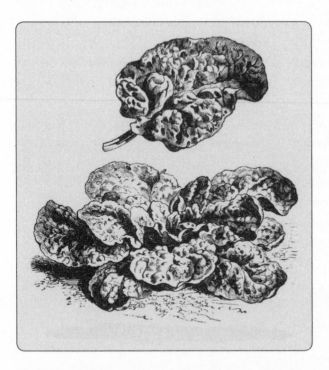

Whisk together Homemade Tahini, soy sauce, and agave nectar in a small bowl and reserve.

Prepare an ice water bath in a very large bowl. Bring a very large pot of water to a rolling boil. Submerge spinach and basil leaves in boiling water until wilted, 1 minute. Drain in a colander and quickly transfer to ice water bath for 2 to 3 minutes to preserve green color. Using your hands, squeeze all excess water from spinach and basil 3 times and reserve in a bowl.

Pack 3 to 4 tablespoons squeezed spinach and basil into a small (1½-inch) cookie cutter or shot glass; turn out onto a plate and repeat with remaining spinach and basil. Drizzle each spinach/basil bundle with 2 teaspoons of the tahini-soy mixture and sprinkle with sesame seeds.

Butternut Squash Curry with Jasmine Rice

Serves 4

Come autumn, our local Amish produce auction sells butternut squash by the wagonload to folks in the Ozarks who are eager to start baking squash pies and other dishes. When I see those beautiful red baskets filled with butternut, all I can think of is my favorite comfort food—curry. At the restaurant, we use butternut squash throughout the winter months to make this wonderful dish, which always receives rave reviews.

4 tablespoons coconut oil, divided

1 large onion, thinly sliced

6 garlic cloves, thinly sliced

1 stalk lemongrass, tough outer layers removed, trimmed and chopped into 2-inch pieces

1 tablespoon peeled and minced fresh ginger

1 2-pound butternut squash, peeled, seeded, and cubed (about 5 cups)

1 red bell pepper, seeded and sliced into thin strips

1 yellow bell pepper, seeded and sliced into thin strips

1 14.5-ounce can coconut milk

¼ cup water, plus more if necessary

3 tablespoons No-Fish Fish Sauce (recipe, page 179)

2 tablespoons vegetarian red curry paste

2 teaspoons agave nectar

2 Thai red chilies, thinly sliced (remove seeds for milder curry)

1 cup shredded Thai basil leaves, plus more for garnish

Cooked jasmine rice

Heat 2 tablespoons oil in a large, heavy, high-sided skillet or wok over medium heat. Add onions, garlic, lemongrass, and ginger and cook over medium heat until fragrant and onions are translucent, 4 to 5 minutes. Remove from skillet and reserve.

Add remaining oil and cook squash, stirring occasionally, until soft, 10 to 12 minutes. Add reserved onion mixture and peppers and cook, stirring, until peppers begin to soften, 3 to 4 minutes.

Add coconut milk, water, No-Fish Fish Sauce, curry paste, agave nectar, and chilies. Bring to a boil, reduce heat, and simmer until heated through, 5 to 6 minutes, adding basil during last 2 minutes of cooking. Remove from heat and remove lemongrass pieces.

Serve over jasmine rice, garnished with additional basil.

Butternut Squash Ravioli

Makes 28 to 30 ravioli

Making pasta by hand may be labor-intensive, but it sure is worth it. This pliant, cooperative dough gets its elasticity from a touch of olive oil, a light knead, and some resting time. If you don't feel like making the dough by hand, use 4-inch round or square wonton wrappers from the refrigerator case at the grocery store. They won't have quite the rustic nature of our ravioli, but they'll do. Our filling of choice is sweet butternut squash balanced with onion, garlic, and herbs—but use your imagination and fill with all manner of vegetable combinations.

Dough
1 cup all-purpose flour
1 cup semolina flour
½ teaspoon salt
½ cup water
2 tablespoons olive oil

Filling
2 cups cubed butternut squash

2 tablespoons olive oil
½ cup minced onion
1 clove minced garlic
1½ tablespoons nutritional yeast
1 teaspoon chopped fresh marjoram
1 teaspoon finely chopped rosemary
½ teaspoon salt
¼ teaspoon freshly ground black pepper
Water for sealing ravioli

Make ravioli:
Pulse together all-purpose flour, semolina, and salt in food processor fitted with the metal blade. Add water and olive oil and process until a firm dough just forms, 15 to 20 seconds. Transfer to a lightly floured surface and knead lightly for 1 minute until dough is even firmer. Divide into 6 equal-sized pieces, wrap in plastic wrap, and refrigerate for at least 30 minutes and up to 8 hours.

Make filling:
Place butternut squash in a steamer basket and steam until tender, 18 to 20 minutes. Pass through a food mill and reserve.

   While squash is cooking, heat oil in a small sauté pan over medium heat. Add onions and cook, stirring, until golden, 8 to 9 minutes. Add garlic and cook an additional minute. Remove from heat and cool. Combine with squash puree, yeast, marjoram, rosemary, salt, and pepper and reserve.

Fill and cook ravioli:

Place a large stockpot on the stove filled with salted water and bring to a boil.

Remove one piece of dough from refrigerator and unwrap. Set the dial on a hand-crank pasta maker to the highest setting. Roll dough through pasta maker, fold dough in half widthwise then roll again at highest setting. Decrease the setting and repeat at each setting to form a very long, thin rectangle, like a large piece of lasagna (about 20 inches long by 5 inches wide). Repeat with a second portion of dough and place both on a lightly floured surface. Brush the outer edges of one piece with water mixture. Spoon 1 tablespoon filling onto pasta 7 or 8 times, leaving about 2½ inches between each spoonful. Cover with second piece of pasta. Starting at one end, press the air out of the dough and seal around the filling. Press out circles with a 3-inch round cookie cutter and crimp edges with a fork or your fingers. Repeat with remaining dough.

Place ravioli in uncovered stockpot and boil until pasta floats to the top, 1 to 2 minutes. Serve with Tomato and Shallot Sauce (recipe page 165).

Heirloom Spaghetti Squash with Heirloom Tomato Spaghetti Sauce

Serves 8

Believed to have originated in China, this marvelous-looking squash was first introduced in Japan by the Sakata Seed Company in 1934. The most labor-intensive part of this recipe is cutting open the spaghetti squash. You need a big, sharp knife and some patience. Instead of steaming or boiling, brush the cut sides with olive oil, salt, and pepper, lay facedown on a baking sheet, and let the oven do most of the work. The cooking method helps the squash develop flavor as it bakes. The reward? Seeds that you can plant for next year's crop, plus the stringy, spaghetti-like strands that soak up our delicious bell pepper–studded spaghetti sauce.

Squash

1 large spaghetti squash (2½ pounds)
3 tablespoons olive oil, divided
1½ teaspoons salt, divided
¼ teaspoon freshly ground black pepper

Sauce

2 pounds ripe heirloom tomatoes, such as Jersey Giant, San Marzano, or Mama Leone

¼ cup olive oil, divided
1 small onion, finely chopped
1 green bell pepper, seeded and finely chopped
2 cloves garlic, crushed
¼ cup fresh basil leaves, chopped (about 2 tablespoons)
1 teaspoon chopped fresh marjoram
1 teaspoon salt
¼ teaspoon freshly ground black pepper

Roast squash:

Preheat oven to 375°F. Using a heavy knife, split squash lengthwise and scoop out the seeds (reserve seeds for planting or toasting). Brush tops of squash halves with olive oil and sprinkle with 1 teaspoon salt. Place squash halves cut-side down on a baking sheet and bake until shell can be pierced, 30 to 40 minutes. Remove squash from oven, scoop inside from end to end to release strands, discard shells, and place strands on a serving platter.

Make sauce:

While squash is roasting, working in batches, blanch tomatoes in boiling water for 45 seconds.

Remove with a slotted spoon and place in a colander to cool. Remove skins (tomatoes should slip from skins easily) and puree in a food processor or blender, 10 to 15 seconds. (If you prefer your sauce chunky, chop up tomatoes with a knife.)

Heat 2 tablespoons olive oil in a 4-quart saucepan over medium-high heat. Add onions and peppers and cook, stirring occasionally, until peppers have softened and onions are translucent, 8 minutes. Add garlic and cook an additional minute.

Add crushed tomatoes, basil, marjoram, salt, and pepper, and bring to a boil. Reduce heat and simmer until sauce is reduced by one third, 15 to 20 minutes.

Toss roasted squash with remaining olive oil, salt, and pepper, and top with sauce.

Sweet Dumpling Winter Squash with Apple, Cranberry, and Walnut Stuffing

Serves 10

I love autumn and the squash harvest. During the summer months, I wait with great anticipation while our squash grows and the colors transition as the seasons change. Eventually the vines die, and the vast variety of our homegrown winter squash starts to peek out between the brown leaves and dried vine. Sweet Dumpling squash is quite prolific, and its size is perfect for single servings of one of my family's favorite desserts. You can't beat the taste of heirloom squash paired with freshly picked apples, which makes this dish especially popular at our restaurant.

10 Sweet Dumpling winter squash or small acorn squash (about 10 ounces each)

4 large baking apples (about 2 pounds), such as Ida Reds or Macintosh, cored and cut into ¼-inch cubes

½ cup turbinado sugar

½ cup Sucanat

¾ cup chopped walnuts

¾ cup dried cranberries

½ cup coconut oil

1½ teaspoons cinnamon

½ teaspoon nutmeg

Preheat oven to 350°F.

Cut top off of each squash, taking care to leave the stem intact; reserve tops.

With a spoon, scoop out seeds and either discard or dry for later use. Place each squash, cut-side down, in a 9- x 13-inch baking dish and fill with ¼ inch water. Cover with foil.

Place the tops in a pie plate filled with ¼ inch water and cover with foil as well. Bake both until softened but still firm, 30 to 35 minutes.

While squash is baking, combine apples, sugar, Sucanat, walnuts, cranberries, coconut oil, cinnamon, and nutmeg in a large bowl.

When squash is done, remove from oven and set squash tops aside. Using tongs, turn squash right side up and fill each squash with about ½ to ¾ cup apple mixture. Cover with foil and bake until tender, an additional 30 to 35 minutes.

Serve squash with their tops as a garnish.

Japanese Yam Gnocchi with Miso-Scallion Sauce

Serves 6 to 8 as an appetizer or 4 as a main course

Unlike other sweet potatoes, which stay very moist when cooked, Japanese yams are almost powdery-dry, with a yellow interior that's somewhere in color between a Yukon Gold potato and a parsnip. To sauce these gnocchi, we stuck with our favorite Asian flavors and created a creamy miso-scallion sauce that clings to the moist dumplings to create a dish that's simultaneously comforting and surprising.

2 pounds Japanese sweet potatoes, scrubbed

1 cup (or more) all-purpose flour

2 teaspoons Ener-G egg replacer, combined with 2 tablespoons warm water

1 teaspoon nutritional yeast

1 teaspoon coarse kosher salt

⅛ teaspoon freshly grated nutmeg

1 tablespoon vegetable oil

1½ cups unsweetened almond milk

3½ tablespoons blond miso paste (or more to taste)

2 chopped scallions, plus more for garnish

Preheat oven to 400°F. Pierce sweet potatoes all over with a fork, wrap individually in foil, and bake until soft, about 60 to 70 minutes. Unwrap and cool potatoes until they can be handled, then cut them in half.

Working in batches, scoop hot potato flesh into a potato ricer. Rice potatoes into a large bowl. Add flour and toss to coat.

Form a well in the center of the potato mixture. Add reconstituted egg replacer, nutritional yeast, salt, nutmeg, and oil. Stir with fork, being careful not to overprocess, until mixture is evenly moistened (mixture will look shaggy).

Turn mixture out onto a lightly floured work surface. Knead just until dough comes together (again, do not overprocess), sprinkling dough with flour very lightly only if dough is very sticky.

Bring a large pot of salted water to a boil.

Form dough into a ball and divide into 4 pieces. On a lightly floured work surface, roll each piece with hands into a ½-inch-thick rope.

Using a bench scraper or knife, cut each rope into ½-inch pieces. Crimp each piece gently with a fork if desired. Transfer gnocchi to prepared baking sheets as you cut them.

Working in batches, cook gnocchi in water until gnocchi rise to surface of water, 1 to 2 minutes, being careful not to overcook.

Using a slotted spoon, carefully transfer gnocchi to a bowl and reserve ¼ cup cooking liquid.

Bring almond milk to a low boil in a large, high-sided skillet. Add miso and whisk until blended. Add gnocchi and scallions, and toss to coat over low heat, adding reserved cooking liquid by the tablespoon if necessary to thicken sauce. Garnish with additional scallions if desired and serve immediately.

Creamy Jerusalem Artichoke Soup with Crispy Chips

Serves 6 to 8

These roots look like a cross between ginger and potatoes, but have a distinct, nutty-crisp flavor and texture. They're neither artichokes nor from Jerusalem, but since they're a relative of the sunflower, Italians called them *carciofi girasole*—"sunflower artichokes." Since *girasole* sounds something like Jerusalem, this unique vegetable came to be named after the Middle Eastern city. We like cooking it down, pureeing it into soup, and topping it with crispy chips that add toasty contrast.

2 pounds Jerusalem artichokes	½ teaspoon salt
2 tablespoons lemon juice	¼ teaspoon freshly ground black pepper
1 cup light olive oil, divided	6 cups vegetable broth or imitation
1 large chopped onion (2 cups)	chicken broth
2 cloves chopped garlic	Chopped chives for garnish

Fill a large bowl halfway with cold water and add lemon juice. Peel Jerusalem artichokes, roughly chop, and place in lemon water to prevent discoloration.

Heat 2 tablespoons oil in a large saucepan over medium-high heat. Add onions and cook, stirring, until translucent, 7 to 8 minutes. Add garlic and cook an additional minute. Drain all but 1 large Jerusalem artichoke from lemon water, add to pot with salt and pepper, and cook, stirring, until artichokes begin to soften, about 5 minutes. Add broth, bring to a boil, reduce heat, and simmer until artichokes are tender, 45 to 50 minutes.

While soup is cooking, heat remaining oil over medium-high heat until hot but not smoking, about 350°F. While oil is heating, pat remaining Jerusalem artichoke dry. Use a mandolin slicer or knife to slice the artichoke as thinly as possible. Working in batches, fry slices until golden brown, 1 minute. Remove with a slotted spoon and drain on paper towels.

Working in batches, transfer soup to a blender and puree until smooth. Return to saucepan and cook until warmed through, 3 to 4 minutes. Divide among bowls and top with Jerusalem artichoke chips. Garnish with chives.

"Put Up" Tomatoes

Makes 4 quarts

After mastering this basic recipe for preserving summer tomatoes, you'll never panic at the prospect of a bumper crop again. Removing the skins from the tomatoes makes them silky and versatile. And of course, the riper the better. Since there is some controversy about the amount of acid needed to keep preserving tomatoes safe using the water bath method, we always add acid. That being said, some varieties of tomatoes—such as Purple Calabash—have a higher level of natural acidity, so in such cases, you may slightly reduce the addition of lemon juice at your own discretion.

10 pounds heirloom tomatoes (any variety)
2 teaspoons non-iodized canning or kosher salt
½ cup fresh lemon juice

Bring a large pot of water to a boil. When water is boiling, set up an ice water bath in a large bowl.

Using a paring knife, cut an "✗" into the bottom of each tomato. Five or six at a time, drop tomatoes into boiling water for 30 seconds. Using a slotted spoon, transfer tomatoes to ice water bath for 1 minute. Slip tomatoes from skins, discard skins, and place tomatoes in a large bowl.

If tomatoes are large (4 inches or more in diameter), quarter them; if medium (2 to 3 inches), halve them. If small, leave them whole. Toss tomatoes with their juice and add salt.

Strain tomatoes of their juice, reserving juice.

Pack tomatoes in hot sterilized quart jars, leaving as little space in between tomatoes as possible and ½ inch headspace at top of jars. Pour tomato juice evenly among jars, topping off with water if necessary to fill to top of tomatoes. Run a spatula or knife around edge of jar to release air bubbles. Carefully pour 2 tablespoons lemon juice on top of tomatoes and juice, leaving ½ inch headspace at tops of jars. Wipe rims of jars, then seal with caps and lids. Process in a water bath canner for 60 minutes. Remove from water and cool completely before labeling. Tomatoes can be used immediately.

Tomato-Tomatillo Tortilla Soup

Serves 6

I'm not one to cast aspersions on tomato soup, but sometimes a little variety is in order. By adding in tart tomatillos and roasting them along with the heirloom tomatoes, we came up with a smoky, tangy, personality-filled soup. Use any kind of tomatoes you have on hand—the sweet and flavorful Emerald Evergreen works really well if you want your soup mostly green, but you can also experiment by using other colors, like orange and the more traditional red. This is also a perfect venue for overripe tomatoes, since they get roasted and pureed anyway. If you can't find tomatillos, feel free to use all tomatoes in this recipe. If you do, add a generous squeeze of lime juice to give the soup its signature zippy tang. We included the crunchy tortilla strips to add even more intrigue—layer them on top of bowls of soup for a crunchy surprise.

3 small white or yellow non-GMO, organic corn tortillas

5 tablespoons olive oil, divided

1½ teaspoons salt, divided

2½ pounds medium heirloom tomatoes, cored and halved

1 pound large tomatillos, papery outer husks removed, rinsed, dried, cored, and halved

1 medium onion, outer skin removed, cut into 1-inch-thick wedges

½ teaspoon freshly ground black pepper

2 large cloves garlic, peeled

3 cups vegetable stock

1 teaspoon ground cumin

¼ teaspoon chili flakes

Diced avocado, chopped cilantro, lime wedges, and finely diced red onion for garnish

Preheat oven to 450°F. Brush tortillas with 1½ tablespoons oil and sprinkle with ½ teaspoon salt. Using a sharp knife or pizza cutter, slice tortillas into ¼-inch strips. Arrange on a baking sheet and bake until lightly browned and crisp, 6 to 7 minutes. Remove from oven and reserve.

Raise oven temperature to 475°F. Divide tomatoes, tomatillos, and onions between 2 large cookie sheets, brush with 3 tablespoons olive oil, and sprinkle with remaining salt and ½ teaspoon pepper. Place garlic cloves in the center of a 5-inch square of aluminum foil and drizzle with remaining ½ tablespoon oil. Seal tightly and place on one of the 2 cookie sheets.

Place in oven and roast until tomatoes have collapsed and edges are charred, 30 to 35 minutes, removing garlic after 20 minutes. Let vegetables cool slightly, then transfer to a 4-quart saucepan and add stock, cumin, and chili flakes. Bring to a boil, reduce heat, and cook until liquid has reduced by about 2 inches, 10 to 15 minutes. Remove from heat. Using an immersion blender, carefully blend soup until partially smooth but still chunky. Serve with avocado, cilantro, lime wedges, red onion, and reserved tortilla strips.

Tomato and Melon Salad

Serves 6

It's incredible how well lush, ripe tomatoes marry with juicy, at-its-peak melon. In fact, there are certain times of the year when they're almost hard to tell apart if you close your eyes and let your taste buds be your guide—after all, tomatoes are indeed a fruit. Although we typically make this salad with sweet and flavorful tomatoes, like the bicolored Pineapple or Dr. Wyche's Yellow, feel free to play around with the combination as you see fit. The challenge here is to use the ripest, juiciest produce you can get your hands on.

4 tablespoons light olive oil

6 tablespoons white balsamic vinegar

½ teaspoon freshly ground black pepper

¼ teaspoon salt

2 tablespoons chopped fresh mint, plus
   more for garnish

2 pounds heirloom tomatoes, such as
   Pineapple or Dr. Wyche's Yellow, cut
   into chunks

1 small orange melon (about 1½ pounds),
   such as Charentais, seeded

¼ cup thinly sliced red onion

Whisk oil, vinegar, pepper, salt, and mint in a bowl.

Combine tomatoes, melon, and onion in a serving bowl and gently toss with dressing.

Garnish with additional mint.

Tomato and Shallot Sauce

Makes 5 cups

Using shallots in this sauce lends a mellower flavor that differentiates it from most onion-based sauces. San Marzano tomatoes, usually considered the gold standard of canned tomatoes, are even more incredible fresh from the garden. Use this as a dipping sauce for hot garlicky bread sticks, with our Breaded Heirloom Eggplant Cutlets (recipe page 77), or with cooked pasta for lunch or a light dinner.

3 pounds ripe San Marzano or other heirloom tomatoes

¼ cup olive oil

1 pound shallots, finely chopped (about 2½ cups)

10 cloves crushed garlic

2 teaspoons salt

1 cup chopped fresh basil

Bring 4 quarts of water to a boil in a 6-quart pot and set up an ice water bath in a large bowl.

Using a paring knife, cut an "✕" into the bottom of each tomato. Five or six at a time, drop tomatoes into boiling water for 30 seconds. Using a slotted spoon, transfer tomatoes to ice water bath for 1 minute. Slip tomatoes from skins and discard skins.

Stem and core tomatoes, and puree in a food processor or blender until smooth, 15 to 20 seconds. Drain water from pot so you can reuse it.

Heat oil in same pot over medium-high heat. Add shallots and cook until slightly translucent, 4 to 5 minutes. Add garlic and cook an additional minute. Add crushed tomatoes and bring to a boil. Reduce heat and simmer, uncovered, stirring occasionally, until sauce is thickened, about 30 minutes. Remove from heat, add salt and basil, and stir to incorporate.

Sauce can be made 72 hours in advance and refrigerated before use, or frozen for up to 1 month.

Tomato Gravy

Makes 3 cups

This traditionally Southern sauce is so simple. Blending it gives it a silky texture similar to a traditional gravy, making it incredibly versatile in the kitchen. Use a workhorse sauce heirloom like Cherokee Purple or the mildly acidic Goldman's Italian-American.

2 pounds heirloom tomatoes, cored and chopped (about 4 cups)

2 teaspoons vegan imitation chicken seasoning

2 tablespoons olive oil

¼ cup flour

¾ teaspoon onion powder

¼ teaspoon garlic powder

Combine tomatoes and imitation chicken seasoning in a blender or food processor and puree until smooth; reserve.

Heat oil in a skillet until hot but not smoking. Add flour and cook, whisking constantly, until a paste is formed and is light brown and toasty, 2 to 3 minutes.

Next, whisk tomatoes, onion powder, and garlic powder into flour mixture. Bring to a boil, reduce heat, and simmer until thickened, 5 to 6 minutes.

Fresh Tomato Sauce

Makes about 4 cups

This type of fresh tomato sauce can be found all over Italy, where cooks in both restaurants and homes understand that as long as the star ingredient—tomatoes—can stand on its own, the rest doesn't need much embellishment. Try adapting the type of heirloom tomato you use here, switching in more or less acidic or sweet varieties according to your taste and what's available in your garden or your local farmers' market. This recipe also works well with deep purple tomatoes, which have a complex, earthy flavor.

2 tablespoons olive oil
¾ cup minced shallots
5 cloves garlic, minced
2 cups diced yellow heirloom tomatoes
2 cups diced green heirloom tomatoes
¼ cup minced fresh basil, plus more for
    garnish

½ teaspoon salt
¼ teaspoon freshly ground black pepper
½ teaspoon fresh crumbled sage
Cooked angel hair pasta

Heat olive oil in a medium saucepan over medium-low heat. Add shallots and cook, stirring, until translucent but not browned, 4 to 5 minutes. Add garlic and cook an additional minute.

Transfer to a medium bowl and toss with tomatoes, basil, salt, pepper, and sage. Serve over angel hair pasta and garnish with additional basil.

Fried Green Tomatoes

Makes 10 to 12 tomatoes

This is a Southern dish that I think could take over the world. Using firm, under-ripe green tomatoes is the secret here; that way they hold up to their breading and frying with character. Using silken tofu to coat the tomatoes is a revelation, and a technique that can be translated to all manner of other dishes. I love the way the nutritional yeast adds a savory flavor, and the panko crumbs help the cornmeal stay crisp even when cooled and served at room temperature.

Batter
1 12-ounce package firm silken tofu
3 tablespoons water
¼ teaspoon salt

Breading
1 cup vegan panko bread crumbs
½ cup cornmeal
2 tablespoons nutritional yeast flakes
2 teaspoons garlic powder

1 teaspoon turmeric
1 teaspoon onion powder
½ teaspoon salt
¼ teaspoon cayenne pepper

Fried Green Tomatoes
2 large or 3 medium firm underripe
   tomatoes (about 1 pound)
½ cup unbleached all-purpose flour
Vegetable oil for frying

Make batter:
Blend tofu, water, and salt until smooth, and transfer to a shallow dish.

Make breading:
Combine panko, cornmeal, yeast, garlic powder, turmeric, onion powder, salt, and cayenne in a shallow dish.

Fry tomatoes:
Slice tomatoes into ¼-inch-thick rounds and dredge each tomato slice in flour, shaking off excess, then dip in tofu puree. Heat ¼ inch oil in a large cast iron skillet over medium-high heat. Press each tofu-dipped tomato into the breading mixture, pressing firmly so breading sticks. Pan fry tomatoes, flipping until both sides are browned, 2 to 3 minutes per side.

   Serve warm or at room temperature.

Multicolored Virgin Bloody Marys

Makes 8 cups total

There comes that point in every tomato gardener's bumper crop when there are simply too many tomatoes to handle. When you've had enough of sauces and salads, consider turning extra tomatoes into juice—then transforming it into these delicious virgin drinks. It's a great way to use up any color heirloom tomatoes: green, red, or yellow. Adjust the spice to your liking, and if you've chosen to make Pepper Hot Sauce from our master recipe on p. 133, by all means use it here.

1½ pounds very ripe heirloom tomatoes, such as Dr. Wyche's Yellow or Green Zebra

1½ pounds very ripe red heirloom tomatoes, such as Oxheart or Beefsteak

¼ cup fresh lemon juice

¼ cup fresh lime juice

4 tablespoons grated fresh horseradish, divided

1½ tablespoons chipotle hot sauce

1½ tablespoons green hot pepper sauce

2 tablespoons Vegan Worcestershire Sauce (recipe page 184), divided

2 teaspoons celery salt, divided

Small celery sticks for garnish

Lemon and lime wheels for garnish

Prepare and ice-water bath in a large bowl.

Bring a large pot of water to a boil. Using a paring knife, cut an "✗" into the bottom of each tomato. Drop into water for 30 seconds. Using a slotted spoon, transfer to ice water bath to cool. When cool enough to handle, slip tomatoes out of their skins and transfer to a bowl.

Core all tomatoes. Puree yellow tomatoes until smooth, 30 seconds, then transfer to a quart-sized container.

Puree red tomatoes until smooth, 30 seconds, then transfer to another quart-sized container.

To red tomato puree add ¼ cup lemon juice, 2 tablespoons horseradish, 1 tablespoon Vegan Worcestershire Sauce, the chipotle Tabasco, and 1 teaspoon celery salt. Stir to combine and chill until ready to use.

To yellow tomato purée add ¼ cup lime juice, 2 tablespoons horseradish, 1 tablespoon Vegan Worcestershire Sauce, the green Tabasco, and 1 teaspoon celery salt. Stir to combine and chill until ready to use.

Moisten the rims of small (3 to 4 ounces) cocktail glasses and dip in celery salt. Carefully pour Bloody Mary mixture into glasses. Garnish with celery sticks and lemon and lime wheels.

Zucchini Relish

Makes 6 quarts

This family favorite is a great way to use up extra zucchini, which overwhelms us with its abundance during summer months. My sister, Jessica, created this relish recipe . . . which we truly do relish!

2½ pounds zucchini, grated (about 10 cups)

2 red bell peppers, seeded and grated

2 green bell peppers, seeded and grated

2 medium onions, peeled and grated (4 cups)

1 cup non-iodized canning salt or kosher salt

2½ cups fresh lemon juice

⅓ cup cornstarch

1 teaspoon turmeric

2 cups agave nectar

2 teaspoons dill seed

½ cup chopped fresh dill

Combine zucchini, red and green peppers, onions, and salt in a large, heavy-duty stainless steel pot. Toss well, cover, and refrigerate overnight or up to 16 hours.

Remove pot from refrigerator, uncover, and pour mixture into a large colander to drain. Return relish back to pot and cover with cold water, stirring to release salt. Drain again, and repeat this process 2 more times.

After the third rinse, return relish to colander, then squeeze out as much excess liquid as you can by placing relish in batches into a clean kitchen towel, folding towel, and twisting from both ends to extract excess liquid. Return relish to pot. In a small bowl, combine lemon juice, cornstarch, and turmeric until smooth, then add agave nectar and dill seed.

Add to relish, stir, and bring to a boil. Reduce heat and cook, stirring often, until zucchini is tender and mixture has thickened, 15 minutes, adding fresh dill during the last 5 minutes.

Pour hot relish into 6 hot, sterilized quart jars, leaving ½ inch headspace. Cap and seal jars and process in a water bath canner for 10 minutes.

Remove from water bath and cool completely before labeling.

After 24 hours, check seals and then place in the pantry for a minimum of 2 weeks before opening and serving.

Curry Scones

Makes 8 scones

Who knew a scone could be so savory? These contain Madras curry, which deepens and intensifies the flavor, and the paprika causes the delicate, crumbly interior to turn a compelling shade of red. Instead of having these with hot tea, try them with a glass of mint iced tea. Though the currants add a touch of sweetness, you could push the contrast even further by spreading them with currant or Blackberry Jam (recipe on page 43).

2 cups unbleached all-purpose flour, plus more for flouring work surface

3 tablespoons Sucanat crystals or light brown sugar

1½ tablespoons Madras curry powder

1 tablespoon ground flaxseed

2 teaspoons baking powder

½ teaspoon baking soda

½ teaspoon salt

3 tablespoons very cold coconut oil or vegan margarine, cut into ½-inch cubes

1 teaspoon finely minced garlic

1 teaspoon finely minced ginger

¾ cup coconut milk

½ tablespoon fresh lime juice

3 tablespoons dried currants

½ teaspoon paprika

Preheat oven to 400°F.

Pulse flour, Sucanat, curry powder, flaxseed, baking powder, baking soda, and salt in a food processor until incorporated. Add coconut oil, garlic, and ginger, and pulse until pea-sized lumps form. Add coconut milk and lime juice and pulse until a sticky dough just forms, 20 to 25 pulses, adding currants during last 10 pulses.

Transfer dough to a lightly floured surface and gently pat into an 8-inch circle (about ¾ inch thick), being careful not to overhandle dough. Slice into 8 equal-sized wedges. Place on a parchment paper–lined cookie sheet and sprinkle with paprika. Bake until lightly browned, 14 to 16 minutes.

Sundried Tomato Basil Bread

Makes 2 loaves

When my mother makes this bread—usually during festivals on the farm—guests arrive early and often to Baker Creek to buy every last loaf. Using bread flour makes a big difference, and the coconut oil adds to the bread's richness and tenderness. If you don't have oil-packed tomatoes, use very moist sundried tomatoes and add ¼ cup extra-virgin olive oil.

2½ cups lukewarm water

1 tablespoon active dry yeast

⅓ cup evaporated cane juice crystals, divided

1 cup oil-packed sundried tomatoes, chopped, oil not discarded

¼ cup coconut oil, slightly melted

1½ teaspoons salt

2 tablespoons chopped fresh basil or 2 teaspoons dried

5½ cups bread flour, plus more for kneading

Combine water, yeast, and 1 tablespoon cane juice crystals in a very large bowl and let sit until slightly foamy, 10 minutes.

Add remaining crystals, tomatoes and oil, coconut oil, salt, and basil and stir with a wooden spoon.

Add 4 cups of flour 1 cup at a time, stirring well after each addition, until dough is stiff and difficult to stir. Remove dough to a floured work surface.

Add remaining 1½ cups flour by the half cup and work dough with your hands, kneading until you get a smooth, elastic, soft ball of dough, 5 minutes.

Oil dough lightly, place in a large clean bowl, and cover with plastic wrap. Let rise until doubled, 1½ to 2 hours. Punch down, form into loaves, and place into 2 greased 9- x 5-inch loaf pans.

Let rise again until doubled in size, 45 minutes to 1 hour.

Preheat oven to 350°F. Bake until tops are golden and a skewer inserted into center comes out clean, 35 to 40 minutes.

Remove from pans and place on racks to cool completely.

Pumpkin Poppy Seed Rolls

Makes 24 rolls

A great way to use up all manner of squash, these rolls are best made with plain old pumpkin, which lend the rolls a golden hue and exceedingly moist texture. We've always got poppy seeds on hand, and they add a bit of extra interest and very subtle crunch to an already delicious recipe.

1 pound (about 4 cups) pumpkin, butternut squash, or sweet potatoes, cubed

1 tablespoon active dry yeast

¼ cup warm water

1 cup agave nectar, divided

1¼ cups plain soymilk, warmed

½ cup coconut oil, plus more for greasing
bowl

1½ tablespoons liquid lecithin

2 tablespoons poppy seeds

1½ teaspoons salt

2½ cups unbleached white bread flour,
plus up to 2 more cups if needed

Place pumpkin in a steamer basket and steam until tender, 18 to 20 minutes. Mash with a masher or puree in a food processor until fine; reserve.

Dissolve yeast, water, and 1 teaspoon agave nectar in a bowl and let stand until yeast begins to foam, 5 minutes. Add soymilk and transfer to a large mixing bowl or stand mixer.

Add pumpkin, remaining agave nectar, coconut oil, lecithin, poppy seeds, and salt. Add 2½ cups flour and combine until well incorporated; let rest up to 15 minutes.

Add additional flour ½ cup at a time until a soft dough forms. Transfer to a floured work surface and knead until smooth, 6 to 7 minutes; dough will be very sticky.

Grease a bowl with additional coconut oil, transfer dough to bowl, cover, and allow to rise until doubled in volume, about 2 hours. Punch down, form into about 24 buns, and arrange on 2 large parchment paper–lined cookie sheets; cover lightly.

Allow dough to double in size again, about 1 hour. Preheat oven to 350°F and bake until lightly browned, 25 to 30 minutes.

Choc-Coco Ice Cream

Makes 4 cups

I love a good bowl of ice cream as much as the next person, but my daughter, Sasha, is our champion ice cream eater. This ice cream, which has a dense, fudgy texture and yummy chocolate-coconut flavor, is sure to please any chocolate lover.

3 cups coconut milk

¾ cup agave nectar

¼ cup unsweetened cocoa powder

2 tablespoons tapioca starch or
 arrowroot powder, dissolved in
 2 tablespoons water

1 tablespoon vanilla extract

⅛ teaspoon salt

½ cup chopped semisweet chocolate
 or semisweet chocolate chips

Chocolate shavings and toasted coconut
 flakes for garnish

Combine coconut milk, agave nectar, cocoa, tapioca starch, vanilla, and salt in a saucepan and bring to a low boil, whisking, until cocoa is dissolved. Remove from heat and stir in chocolate, whisking until smooth.

Transfer to a bowl and press plastic wrap onto surface of liquid. Chill in refrigerator until very cold, 6 to 8 hours or overnight. Freeze in an ice cream maker according to manufacturer's instructions.

Garnish with chocolate shavings and coconut flakes.

Coconut Whipped Cream

Makes 1½ cups

A can of coconut milk is a workhorse in our kitchen. We use it in everything from curries and casseroles to all kinds of desserts. For this creamy whipped topping, coconut milk gets chilled, which separates the rich, dense solids from the thinner—but still delicious—liquid. Whip up the solids with a few ingredients you probably already have on hand for a dessert topping that might make you forgo the dairy case forever. And don't make the innocent mistake of discarding that liquid—use it for other recipes, such as our Icy Melon, Coconut, and Basil Shake (recipe page 111).

1 15-ounce can full-fat coconut milk
3 to 4 tablespoons powdered sugar, or to taste
1 tablespoon potato starch
½ teaspoon vanilla extract

Place unopened coconut milk can in refrigerator and chill for at least 4 hours.

Open can and carefully remove solidified coconut cream (you will have about ¾ cup solidified cream) from the top; save remaining liquid for another use.

Place coconut cream in the bowl of a stand mixer and whip on high speed until thick, 1 to 2 minutes. Add powdered sugar, potato starch, and vanilla, and whip for an additional minute.

This topping can be made in advance and refrigerated, covered with plastic wrap, for up to 24 hours.

Homemade Graham Crackers

Makes 40 crackers

I grew up eating these rustic, nutty-sweet cookies, and they were a childhood favorite. After tasting them, you'll never want to buy graham crackers again. This healthier version contains three types of flour, natural sweeteners, and no preservatives. These crackers are great with peanut butter and jelly or almond butter, and really versatile in desserts; we crush them to use in our Graham Cracker Pie Crust (recipe page 66), another item we've eliminated from your supermarket shopping list.

1 cup oat flour

1 cup whole wheat pastry flour

1 cup unbleached all-purpose flour

1 cup Sucanat crystals

1 teaspoon baking soda

1 teaspoon cinnamon (optional)

¾ teaspoon salt

1½ sticks vegan buttery sticks, such as Earth Balance, diced and frozen until very hard (at least 30 minutes)

¼ cup dark agave nectar

⅓ cup almond milk, plus more if necessary

1½ tablespoons vanilla extract

Combine flours, Sucanat, baking soda, cinnamon, and salt in a food processor and pulse to incorporate. Add buttery sticks and pulse until a coarse meal forms, 15 pulses. Whisk together agave nectar, almond milk, and vanilla and add to the food processor. Pulse just until a sticky dough forms. Form dough into two ½-inch-thick rectangles, wrap in plastic wrap or wax paper, and chill in refrigerator until hardened, 3 to 4 hours.

Place each hardened rectangle on a sheet of parchment-lined 12- x 17-inch rimless cookie sheet and cover with a sheet of wax paper. Roll to ⅛-inch thickness to edges of cookie sheet. Return to refrigerator and chill an additional 45 minutes to 1 hour.

Preheat oven to 350°F. Remove chilled dough from refrigerator and carefully remove wax paper layer from top. Using a cookie cutter or sharp knife, cut 5 equally spaced straight horizontal lines in rectangle of dough, making 5 equal-sized strips of dough. Cut 8 equally spaced vertical lines; you should have 40 crackers per sheet.

Return to refrigerator and chill an additional 15 minutes.

Bake until golden brown, 20 to 25 minutes. Remove from oven and cool completely. Peel from parchment paper and serve.

Graham crackers can be stored in an airtight container for up to 1 week, or in the freezer for up to 1 month.

Homemade Tahini

Makes about 3 cups

Both Japanese and Middle Eastern cuisines use sesame paste in one form or another. Sure, you could buy it—but why, when it's this easy to make yourself? Just make sure to use the freshest sesame seeds you can get your hands on, plus sesame oil that's been stored in a cool, dry place. And make sure to use pure sesame oil that's light in color; not the dark brown, toasted oil used as a flavor finish in many Asian dishes.

4 cups sesame seeds
¾ cup sesame oil (not toasted), plus more if necessary

Combine sesame seeds and oil in blender and puree until very smooth, 3 to 5 minutes, adding additional oil if necessary, until tahini forms a very thick paste similar in texture to very thick pancake batter.

Transfer to an airtight container. Tahini keeps, refrigerated, in an airtight container for up to 2 months.

No-Fish Fish Sauce

Makes 1 cup

Fish sauce is such an essential part of many of my favorite Asian dishes. In Vietnam, it's mostly made on one tiny island called Phu Quoc, where anchovies and salt are packed into wooden barrels to ferment for months. Because I'm a vegan, fish sauce's core ingredient—fermented anchovies—is off-limits for me. This recipe uses wakame (a type of sea vegetable) and dried mushrooms. To duplicate the mouthwatering *umami* taste the salty, fishy original nails so perfectly, we use a great product called liquid aminos that often has less additives than soy sauce. Save the mushrooms and seaweed after cooking and use them as the base for a great soup.

5 cups water
1 cup dried porcini or shiitake mush-
    rooms or mushroom medley
1 cup shredded wakame (seaweed)

5 cloves garlic, smashed
1 teaspoon whole peppercorns
½ cup liquid aminos (available at health
    food stores)

Combine water, mushrooms, wakame, garlic, and peppercorns in a medium saucepan and bring to a boil. Reduce heat and simmer until liquid darkens and reduces by half, 20 to 25 minutes. Remove from heat, strain liquid from solids, and return liquid to pot. Add liquid aminos, return to a simmer, and cook an additional 5 minutes. Cool and store in refrigerator for up to 1 month.

Soy Sour Cream

Makes 2 cups

This staple comes from my aunt Mindy. The secret here is Instant Clear Jel, an instant, vegetarian binding agent you can order online or find at health food stores. We love to use this sour cream on Mexican food, or stirred into borscht or fruit soup.

2 cups unsweetened organic soymilk

¼ teaspoon salt

2 teaspoons liquid lecithin (available at health food stores)

1 teaspoon fresh lemon juice (or ½ teaspoon powdered citric acid)

½ cup plus 2 tablespoons neutral-flavored oil

1½ tablespoons Instant Clear Jel (available from *www.nutsonline.com*)

Combine soymilk, salt, lecithin, and lemon juice in a blender and blend until smooth. With blender on, slowly drizzle in oil and then add the Clear Jel. Pour into a container and chill before use.

Soy Sour Cream can be stored in refrigerator, in an airtight container, for up to 2 weeks.

Sweet Thai Chili Sauce

Makes 1 cup sauce

You'll see this sauce all over Thailand—and back here at home—in a little glass pot with a spoon at virtually every Thai restaurant. We replaced the usual sugar with agave nectar and used a combination of chili flakes and Thai chilies for ease. You can also adjust the thickness of the sauce depending on how much cornstarch you add, and the recipe can easily be doubled or even tripled, depending on how addicted you get!

1 cup light agave nectar

¼ cup unseasoned rice vinegar

1½ teaspoons chili flakes

1 red Thai chili, seeded and finely
  chopped

4 cloves finely minced garlic

1 teaspoon salt

2 teaspoons non-GMO cornstarch,
  dissolved in 1 tablespoon water

Bring agave nectar, vinegar, chili flakes, Thai chili, garlic, and salt to a boil in a small saucepan. Reduce heat and simmer 5 minutes. Whisk in dissolved cornstarch and simmer an additional minute, until slightly thickened. Cool completely, then refrigerate. Will keep refrigerated, in an airtight container, for up to 1 month.

Seitan Loaf

Makes 2 loaves

My family has been making this versatile meat substitute for three generations. Seitan—essentially hand-processed wheat gluten—is very high in protein and is filling and delicious. Depending on how it is used, it can even fool critics of vegan cooking.

Boiling Broth
12 cups hot water
½ cup soy sauce
⅓ cup imitation chicken vegetable
    seasoning powder
6 cloves garlic
1 tablespoon onion powder
2 teaspoons celery seed
1 cup chopped celery
1 cup chopped onion
2 sprigs fresh thyme
2 sprigs fresh rosemary
2 sprigs fresh marjoram

Gluten
4½ cups gluten flour

¾ cup oat flour
¼ cup whole wheat flour
¾ cup finely ground cashews
¼ cup vegan imitation chicken soup
    powder
2 tablespoons onion powder
1 teaspoon garlic powder
About 5 cups very cold water (must be
    cold!)

Loaves
Two 18- x 12-inch lengths prewashed
    muslin, or a triple layer of cheesecloth
    folded into thirds
Four 3-yard lengths kitchen twine

Make broth:
Place all ingredients for broth in a large stockpot. Cover and bring broth to simmer.

Make gluten:
In a large bowl, whisk together the three flours, cashews, soup powder, onion powder, and garlic powder. Add the cold water. Working quickly, begin kneading and working out any lumps in the gluten, preventing it from "knotting" and adding water a little at a time to incorporate all of the dry flour into the loaf. Continue kneading until gluten strands resembling fibrous strings begin to develop within the dough, 10 to 15 minutes.

Make loaves:

Divide gluten into 2 pieces. Spread one piece of muslin on work surface and place one piece of gluten in the center of it and shape into a 12- x 4-inch loaf.

Fold the right and left pieces of muslin in toward the center of the loaf, leaving some slack on the fabric, which will allow the loaf to expand when cooking.

Fold the bottom piece of muslin up and over the loaf and tuck under. Next, bring the top piece of muslin down and tuck under the loaf, completely enclosing the gluten in muslin. Take twine, double it, and lay it under the loaf horizontally. Bring cut ends of string through the loop end and tie in place. Then repeat one more time horizontally and tie to secure with the excess string.

Take another 3-yard length of twine, tie it to the horizontally tied string at one end. Then spirally wrap the string around the loaf, leaving about 1 inch between, and tie off at the opposite end. When you are tying the circumference of the loaf, it can be made taut.

Repeat with remaining loaf.

Place loaves in the simmering pot of broth; loaves will sink to the bottom. Bring broth to a boil, reduce heat to a simmer, and simmer, covered, occasionally running spoon along edges of the pot to allow loaves to rise, 2 hours.

To check doneness, press on loaves with a spoon; if gluten springs back, it is done.

Cool loaves in broth, then strain and reserve broth for use as a soup stock base, or freeze for another use. Loaves can be stored whole or sliced and tightly covered in the refrigerator for 1 week, or in the freezer for 1 month.

Vegan Worcestershire Sauce

Makes 2 cups

Who knew Worcestershire sauce even had anchovies in it? We didn't. This tastes almost like the real thing, just without the fish. If you happen to have mushroom soy sauce around, use in place of soy sauce in this recipe.

2½ cups apple cider vinegar

¾ cup soy sauce (not low-sodium)

⅓ cup agave nectar

1 teaspoon grated fresh ginger

1 teaspoon mustard seed

1½ teaspoons onion powder

2 cloves crushed garlic

2 cinnamon sticks

1 teaspoon black peppercorns

Bring all ingredients to a boil. Reduce heat and simmer vigorously until liquid is reduced by about one-third, about 30 minutes. Cool with solids, then strain solids and store liquid in refrigerator, in an airtight container, for up to 1 month.

Acknowledgments

Throughout the process of creating this cookbook, we have been reunited with family recipes that our ancestors have enjoyed for generations. We continue to savor the food that our great-grandparents produced from the bounty of their own gardens, thanks to carefully preserved heirloom seeds and recipes passed down through the generations. In keeping with this tradition, we've developed some new recipes, many influenced by both global and local flavors.

As the many months have passed in the creation of this book there are several people who have been irreplaceable in its development. We wish to thank Adeena Sussman for her hours of testing, developing, and tasting these recipes; her expertise has been invaluable.

Thanks to the family and friends who have helped compile these recipes from the four corners of our ancestral kitchens: our grandmothers, Opal Hetterle and Nellie Lee; our mothers, Debbie Gettle and Lyn Freie; my sister, Jessica Frerichs, and my aunt, Mindy Breckenridge; and many others who have generously shared recipes with us through the years.

We would also like to thank Ellen Archer, Leslie Wells, Kerri Kolen, Kiki Koroshetz, and the rest of the staff at Hyperion, who have guided us through the creation of this cookbook. The following people were also invaluable: Marc Gerald, Bill Timmsen, Paul Walace, Brian Dunne, Kathy McFarland, Randel A. Agrella, Hannah Shepherd, Anat Abramov Shimoni, and Florence Swick.

Most of all, thanks to our daughter, Sasha, who is always eager to help us in the kitchen. Her smile and honest opinion keeps us pressing toward the mark of preserving heirlooms—and the recipes they've inspired—for future generations.

Index